Ronald T. Hyman is Professor of Education, Graduate School of Education, Rutgers University.

Games, like art, are a translator of experience.

Marshall McLuhan

Whenever we try to trace the origin of a skill or a practice which played a crucial role in the ascent of man, we usually reach the realm of play.

Eric Hoffer

PAPER,

RONALD T. HYMAN

PENCILS, AND PENNIES

Games for Learning and Having Fun

A SPECTRUM BOOK

PRENTICE-HALL, INC., Englewood Cliffs, N.J. 07632

Library of Congress Cataloging in Publication Data

Hyman, Ronald T.
   Paper, pencils, and pennies.

   (A Spectrum Book)
   Includes bibliographical references.
   1. Simulation games in education. 2. Educational games. I. Title.
LB1029.S53H94   793.7   77-1492
ISBN 0-13-648436-0
ISBN 0-13-648428-X pbk.

For my students in 250:506—Simulations in Teaching

© 1977 by Prentice-Hall, Inc., Englewood Cliffs, New Jersey

All rights reserved. No part of this book
may be reproduced in any form or by any means
without permission in writing from the publisher.

A Spectrum Book

10 9 8 7 6 5 4 3 2 1

Printed in the United States of America

Prentice-Hall International, Inc., *London*
Prentice-Hall of Australia Pty. Limited, *Sydney*
Prentice-Hall of Canada, Ltd., *Toronto*
Prentice-Hall of India Priviate Limited, *New Delhi*
Prentice-Hall of Japan, Inc., *Tokyo*
Prentice-Hall of Southeast Asia Pte. Ltd., *Singapore*
Whitehall Books Limited, *Wellington, New Zealand*

Contents

I
WHY AND HOW

1
Introduction: Purposes and Development   3

2
The Advantages of Simulations/Games   9

3
How to Conduct a Simulation/Game 17

II
WHAT

4
Paper and Pencil Word Games 27

5
Penny-Moving Games 51

6
Paper and Pencil Line and Number Games 71

7
Paper, Pencil, Pennies Like the Real World 91

Appendix A: How to Win at NIM 143

Appendix B: Material for Copying 149

Credits

Games and Puzzles Magazine, 11 Tottenham Court Road, London, England, for permission to use "Penny Royal" by Steve Wilson, November, 1974; "Ambush" by Harry Woollerton, December, 1974; "Numerate" by David Parlett, June, 1976.

David W. Johnson and Frank P. Johnson, *Joining Together: Group Theory and Group Skills,* © 1975, pages 355, 318-322. Reprinted by permission of Prentice-Hall, Inc., Englewood Cliffs, N.J. 07632.

Michael Chester and *Simulation/Gaming,* Box 3039, University Station, Moscow, Idaho 83843 for permission to base the simulation/game "Expressway" on their material in the May, 1972, issue.

Toyce Collins and Carolyn Pagel ("Hungry Zenobians") and Tracy Shisler and Cathy DeGisi ("Land Use"), all students in my simulations class at Rutgers University, for their work with me on two original simulation/games.

My thanks and apologies to any other simulation/game designer whose material I have used and to whom I have inadvertently not given credit. Many people have taught me simulation/games; it has often been the case that they themselves did not know the original sources.

I
WHY AND HOW

> All coherent thinking is equivalent to playing a game according to a set of rules.
>
> ARTHUR KOESTLER

> Discoveries about aircraft in flight have been made in wind tunnels.
>
> RICHARD E. BARTON

1

Introduction: Purpose and Development

Whether you are a teacher, a club leader, or a parent, a grandparent, a caring relative, or a friendly neighbor, most likely you can recall a situation where you spent some time with a youngster or small group of youngsters and wished you had available beneficial ways to spend that time. I know that I have been with youngsters—and even adults—and found that conversation lagged as time seemed to pass more slowly each minute. In those situations I felt the need of a way to help me actively interact with them so that I wouldn't miss an opportunity to share a meaningful experience with them.

Introduction: Purpose and Development

When I thought about the situation, I clearly began to formulate requirements for myself: (1) I wanted a store of activities I could do with other people; (2) I wanted these activities to be simple enough for children yet attractive enough for teenagers and even adults; (3) I wanted each activity to use few materials so that I wouldn't need to carry a loaded suitcase around with me; (4) I wanted the materials for the activity needed materials to be readily available at home or school or recreation center; and (5) I wanted the activities to yield some benefit more than merely passing time, that is, I wanted an educational and/or recreational and/or interpersonal yield from a given activity.

On further consideration I realized that a series of simulation activities and games using only extremely versatile materials would meet my requirements. I found that the most versatile and readily available materials are paper, pencils, and pennies. I could always get my hands on paper and pencils quickly from somebody's desk, especially my own. I could invariably gather together from my pockets and other people's pockets and purses enough pennies to start an exciting simulation or game. I soon stashed away a pile of pennies in a drawer at home for quick and ready use with my children who invariably wanted to play with me when my own pockets were empty.

Think about just pennies for a minute. They can serve as counters just as a chip or a checker, as they slide easily. They have two different sides (a head and a tail), allowing two people to keep their respective pennies apart. Furthermore, with a bit of digging you can even collect and set aside enough pre-1959 pennies to yield pennies for three people to use simultaneously; this is possible because the "tail" of the penny changed in 1959 from the wheat design to the Lincoln Memorial design.

Pennies are durable, allowing you to use the same ones over and over again. And pennies are cheap. Setting aside *even separate* piles at home, school, and club does not require a significant outlay of cash. What is more, you can always regain the full value of the pennies after you're finished using them. Indeed,

Introduction: Purpose and Development

they're virtually perfect materials. Sometimes I even think that the government conceived and designed the penny just for my use.

With thoughts like these I set about collecting simulations/games[1] already described in books and journals. I also designed new ones. Then I used these activities and modified them when necessary to meet my own requirements. Soon I discovered that I had a repertoire of activities that I could call upon at a moment's notice to help me interact with other people effectively and beneficially and to just plain have fun.

The purpose, then, of this book is to provide you with a wealth of ideas for use when you, too, want something different, something special, and something meaningful and enjoyable to fill anywhere from a minute to an hour at home, at school, or at the community center. You can rely on these activities to serve you well for educational, social, and recreational purposes. They're great for good times and learning as well. No longer can you say, "I can't afford simulations and games, so I don't use them." After all, who can't afford and obtain paper, pencils, and a pile of pennies?

This collection of simulations/games includes word games, mathematics games (take-away games and space-capture games), role-playing activities, values-education exercises, and simulations of social and physical situations. Some activities are old ones that you may have seen elsewhere or used already. However, the collection as a whole is fresh and different.

For easy use I have divided the collection into four parts:

Paper and pencil word games

Penny-moving games

Paper and pencil line and number games

Paper, pencil, pennies—like the real world

---

[1]Throughout this book I shall use the term simulations/games as an inclusive general term to refer to simulations, games, simulation games, and other closely related activities. This is in keeping with the usage of other authors as well as the title of a respected journal in the field.

Introduction: Purpose and Development

Naturally, some activities could fit into two of these groups if you wanted to split hairs. Nevertheless, I have found that these four categories serve me well to help me get at the type of simulation/game I want for a given situation. You're welcome to regroup the activities in any way you wish.

The format for presentation of the activities allows you to see quickly if the activity is what you can use with a particular person or group at a particular time. For each activity there are the following items when applicable:

Name of the Simulation/Game
Benefit/Purpose
Materials
Number of Participants
Step-by-Step Procedure
Winner
Example
Variations
Note/Comment
Debriefing Hints

Because I am interested in activities I can engage in with other people in a reciprocal way to heighten our mutual involvement and because I am interested in activities not otherwise readily available in print, I have not included here crossword puzzles, other word puzzles, and drill exercises for learning arithmetic, or spelling, or geography. Each activity here allows and encourages people to interact during it, which is important and necessary. There is no question at all in education today that the learning of facts by themselves is not particularly beneficial. Rather, facts are to be learned along with the learning of concepts, generalizations, and the process of problem-solving. The interaction of people in activities is the part which energizes people to learn facts, concepts, generalizations, and processes in a meaningful context.

Introduction: Purpose and Development

You will note that two crucial elements appear for each activity: (1) a step-by-step procedure to lead you in performing the activity and (2) some hints for debriefing the activity so that you can reap its benefit. The debriefing hints are specific ideas for that activity that go along with a general debriefing strategy explained in the section entitled "How to Conduct a Simulation/Game." (See page 17. Once you familiarize yourself with the general debriefing strategy, which experience tells us is both necessary and effective for benefiting from a simulation/game, then the specific debriefing hints will suffice for each activity. By following the activity's step-by-step procedure and then its debriefing hints you will be able to get going easily and to have a focus for talking afterwards.

I trust that you will enjoy these simulations/games as I have. I trust that you will send me some of your own activities for my use and sharing with other people who are also eager for ideas on interacting beneficially with other people.

> When children are removed from the emotionally charged context in which conflicts usually occur, they are likely to come to an intellectual understanding of what is going on.
>
> JOSIE CRYSTAL

> We ought to be grateful that simulations and games can help us examine and understand the important and pervasive experience of competition itself.
>
> R. GARRY SHIRTS

2

The Advantages Of Simulation/Games

WHY PEOPLE PLAY

Since I am writing this book for both professionals and lay people, many of you will want to know the justifications and advantages of simulations/games. Therefore, I'm offering a chapter on this topic for those of you who are interested in pursuing it more deeply. If you are not, then feel free to go right on to the next chapter, which is devoted to the conducting of simulations/games themselves.

People play because they enjoy doing so. People derive pleasure and satisfaction from play. Play is normal. Every society in the world has play as an integral part of its culture. Children and

The Advantages of Simulation/Games

youth spend a good portion of their developing years in play activities. Play is also important to adults who spend much less time at it than they probably should.

We expect children to play and are pleased when they are playing happily. Children all over engage in mimetic play, that kind of play in which they act out the roles of people they see in their daily lives, or read about in books, or learn about from television and radio. Their role-playing is healthy, for it gives them the opportunity to practice certain skills and learn about life. Children, for example, play house, school, doctor and nurse, cowboys and Indians, cops and robbers, and army. They play with dolls, hobbyhorses, costumes, model trains, toy trucks, and cap pistols. Through role playing activities children internalize the skills of their society. John Dewey, surely the most well-known and respected educational philosopher of this century, claims that the "numberless" spontaneous activities of children, plays, games, mimic efforts, even the apparently meaningless motions of infants" are the "foundation-stones of educational method."[1]

Given the realization of the importance and centrality of play in our lives it is up to us adults who wish to foster healthy growth in children to encourage our youngsters to play. Better yet, it is wise to engage in play with children, the better to observe and understand them. Socrates, when talking about the education of the free man over 2,000 years ago, said "train them by a kind of game, and you will be able to see more clearly the natural bent of each."[2]

THE JUSTIFICATIONS

If you are a skeptic, obviously you want and need more evidence concerning the advantages of simulations/games. Just a quick consideration of common activities in our lives shows that simula-

[1] John Dewey, *The Child and the Curriculum* and *The School and Society* (combined edition). (Chicago: The University of Chicago Press), p. 117.
[2] Plato, *Great Dialogues of Plato*. Translated by W.H.D. Rouse (New York: Mentor, 1956), p. 336.

The Advantages of Simulation/Games

11

tions/games are quite popular and well accepted. For example, astronauts train for their space flights through intensive use of simulations, law students learn through moot court, airplane pilots and auto drivers learn on simulators derived from the Link Trainers of World War II, and first-aid people practice cardiopulmonary resuscitation (CPR) for heart attack and drowning victims with an inflatable dummy called "Resusci-Annie."

A recent newspaper article (*N.Y. Times,* June 18, 1976, p. 81) featured an exclusive new motoring course offered at a Long Island car racing track. The course focuses on tactics in evasive and protective automobile driving. The course teaches security agents how to protect government and corporate officials from kidnappers, terrorists, and assassins. Through simulations the security agents learn, for example, how to cope with roadblocks and how to usher an official to a waiting airplane by car.

Another example from the newspaper appears on the first page of the business section (*New York Times,* February 16, 1977). The story and photograph feature "the most advanced simulator in existence," a simulation in New York City of an oil tanker entering the Milford Haven harbor in Wales. The tanker captains stand on a training bridge of a ship complete with radiotelephone and radar. They watch a panoramic view of the harbor created by three television cameras and a complex of mirrors and coordinated by a small computer. The captains learn how to guide the ship into the harbor under varying conditions such as a hurricane, a mechanical breakdown, a fog, or a holiday when tugboats are unavailable to help them. The headlines of the story indicates the sophisticated nature of the double simulation: *Make-Believe Tanker Enters a Simulated Port.*

Some simulations are even required by law, obviously because our legislators are convinced of the effectiveness of such learning. For example, school children in New Jersey must engage in fire drills—simulated fire-emergency evacuation of the school building—by state law at least twice a month. That is, the law requires simulation. Similarly, students who travel to school on buses simulate bus evacuation by law in New Jersey. Passengers

The Advantages of Simulation/Games

on ocean liners must participate in lifeboat drills, which are simulations. When I was in elementary school during World War II, I participated in many air-raid drills in school, where we simulated an enemy bomber attack on Chicago.

There is much evidence around us to support simulations once we become sensitive to the fantastically high incidence of simulations in our complex lives. For clarity's sake we can categorize the advantages and justifications for simulations under four general headings.[3]

PRESENTING MATERIAL

A simulation/game allows a leader to present material to participants on three levels simultaneously: *facts* about the issue at hand as expressed in the scenario; *processes and skills* that the participants must engage in because the dynamics of the simulation/game call for them to do so; and *alternative strategies* of decision-making that the participants develop as they seek to play and interact with other people. These three levels can go on and do go on simultaneously during a simulation/game because each participant faces not an abstract idea but rather a concrete example of facts, processes, and strategies.

Furthermore, by its very nature the simulation/game through the efforts of the designer clarifies and simplifies a complex process or issue from life. In order to make the simulation/game playable the designer has had to wrestle with simplifying the complex processes of life which he had identified. Through self-effort and consultation with others the designer has developed a simplified, albeit limited, model more easily understandable than the group of real events and processes. This simplified and clarified model facilitates understanding, especially for youngsters who have some difficulty in dealing with complicated and high-level abstractions.

---

[3]I am indebted to Kenneth Oettle for these categories, based in part on some previous writing of mine.

13

The Advantages of Simulation/Games

The simplified model of the simulation/game allows the designer and participants to compress time. We can play for five minutes and let this amount of time represent one half an hour. We can, therefore, conduct a survival exercise or highway-planning session within a single, short simulation/game and thereby present a complete picture to the participant. Without such a compression of time we would not be able to offer a look at or experience a total situation. The view of a total situation provides a context that facilitates the learning of the particular elements of the issue at hand, which otherwise might lose their significance. For example, without knowing what a job interview is like it is difficult for a person to understand the need for a resumé, for references on specific skills required by the employer, or for knowledge of the interviewer's perspective.

As a result of looking to life experiences as the basis of the simulation/game, the designer facilitates the integration of subject matter. That is, a simulation/game seldom, if ever, restricts itself to economics, or biology, or literature, or sociology. Rather, there is an across-subject-matter approach that encourages participants to develop a broad outlook on the issue at hand. To allow this integration to take place, a simulation/game presents a gradual increase of data and rule complexity. The simulation/game does not announce all the rules at once but rather presents the pertinent rules, facts, and events as the play progress. This feature has the added advantage, when tied to the preceding ones, of permitting several people who are at different stages of development or levels of ability to participate together in a common activity just as they do in daily life experiences.

UNBLOCKING

Perhaps the strongest and clearest justification for simulations/games lies in the concept of unblocking. Often there is resistance to learning on the part of a person which he/she may not even be aware of at the moment. There may be a resistance to

The Advantages of Simulation/Games

interacting—verbally or physically—with another person. Simulations/games have the capacity to remove existing barriers to participation because as the activity proceeds the role of the adult leader (teacher, club leader, parent, or whatever) changes from the common one. The leader becomes involved in the activity and hence stimulates and motivates rather than orders and judges. The often-found polarization between teacher and student, club leader and member, and parent and child is reduced.

The interaction among participants—especially when this interaction exists among equals such as students, or club members, or family members—provides the opportunity for a person to learn from someone other than the adult leader. Such peer learning reduces the dependence of the participant on the adult as leader and creates an inter-dependence with the other participant, including the leader if he/she is a participant rather than a director of the activity. This peer interdependence has an educational value that is highly desirable.

In such peer-interdependent situations the participant does not look to the leader as the judge of the performance. Judgment, when existing, is rendered by the rules of the simulation/game and the feedback from other participants. Such judgment is meaningful and less threatening to people than a judgment handed down by the leader.

Unblocking also occurs because the person is no longer a passive recipient of instructions or information but is rather an active and involved participant. The active involvement creates excitement and the subtle but powerful realization by the players that they control their own destiny in the activity. Whereas the realization of powerlessness is paralyzing to players, the realization of control over the decisions directly affecting them is energizing.

Because of the compression of time and the dynamic interaction among participants, players receive rapid feedback about the effectiveness of the decisions they have made. Hence, the usual lag between learning and applying, as well as the lag between

The Advantages of Simulation/Games

deciding and assessing the effectiveness of the decision, virtually disappears in simulations/games. The players benefit from the eliminated lags because they can still vividly recall why and how they decided. Then they can adjust to the changed situation appropriately. Players in this way continually are deciding and assessing and hence learning because there are no barriers to block them.

CHANNELING ENERGIES

People, especially children, are naturally active creatures. All people all over the world play, and simulations/games allow them to direct their energies to a learning situation which is also pleasureful. Simulations/games offer players the opportunity to compete and to cooperate, two modes of behavior everyone faces almost daily. While some people today deemphasize competition and emphasize cooperation, others applaud the teaching of a competitive spirit among people. Nevertheless, whatever your own particular stand on the merits of competition and cooperation, there is no doubt that people must learn to face others who do compete and others who do cooperate.

Simulations/games facilitate opportunities for people to communicate. This is significant given the normal desire of people to communicate with other people. Whereas in a traditional passive setting communication with peers is considered a distraction and a disturbance, in simulations/games the players can channel their communication through partisan positions. People are not naturally neutral beings but rather are for or against an issue, a candidate, or a belief. People take sides, which propels them to continually probe, consider, reassess. The partisan communication during simulations/games is satisfying and beneficial, as it provides practice time with a low threat on what could easily be an unbearable issue.

RESULTS

The Advantages of Simulation/Games

Though the research on smulations/games is still in its infancy, one salient result looms large—simulations/games have a positive effect on the players' attitude toward learning and their motivation. This is shown over and over again in the research and is noted in a recent review of research studies on simulations/games. The authors of the review conclude from the many sources they have studied that "games and simulations appear to have a positive influence on student attitudes . . . . Games and simulations appear to be influential in encouraging students to become more actively involved in the learning process. A teacher trying to involve students in learning can receive considerable aid from the available simulations and games."[4]

In addition to learning the content presented through the simulation/game, players also improve their decision-making ability and their skills of interpersonal interaction because they have the opportunity to practice in concrete form what educators advocate. Players learn that it is good for them to communicate with their peers and not only with the adult in charge—contrary to the unfortunate practice in some school situations. A recent research report in *Psychology Today* (February, 1975) shows that when racial trouble erupted in one Texas city school system, educators and psychologists successfully turned to a simulation/game format to help increase communication and respect among classmates and thus decrease racial tension.

As players communicate and decide, a subtle point surfaces—creativity is desirable and possible. Simulations/games encourage creativity because seldom is only one playing strategy possible or correct. The flexibility of the play tells participants that there are alternatives open to them and that it is up to them to create the desired, successful strategy in achieving their goal. Maybe, just maybe, the most important result of using simulations/games is the motivation toward creative use of our abilities.

[4]Donald R. Wentworth and Darrell R. Lewis, "A Review of Research on Instructional Games and Simulations in Social Studies Education," *Social Education* 37 (1973): 438-439.

> Play in adults as in children is not merely a vacation. It is not merely a lighthearted waste of time, but another order of constructive effort constituting in itself a serious, form-making endeavor.
>
> WILLIAM J.J. GORDON
>
> Just so, in teaching, you must simply work your pupil into such a state of interest in what you are going to teach him that every other object of attention is banished from his mind.
>
> WILLIAM JAMES

3
How to Conduct A Simulation/Game

Two essential elements—flexibility and imagination—underpin the conducting of a simulation/game. These two elements should guide you as you plan, introduce, run, and debrief a simulation/game—whether with one other person or with a group of thirty; whether in school, in the recreation center, or at home; whether with children, youths, or adults. As a leader you need to be sensitive to the various aspects of the activity which require flexible use of space, flexible use of furniture, and flexible groupings of participants. You need to use your imagination because there are no absolute answers regarding such disparate questions as the best use of furniture or the most effective question to ask.

There are, indeed, some general guidelines I strongly suggest that you follow because they will provide a supportive structure as

How to Conduct a Simulation/Game

you move along. Once you are comfortable with simulations/games in general and a given simulation/game in particular, feel free to modify things to suit your specific situation.

Here are some guidelines for conducting a simulation/game. They are in four sections because there are four main parts to conducting a simulation/game, each vital for maximum educational benefit. These parts are: (1) preparing, (2) introducing, (3) running, and (4) debriefing. All four together constitute the conducting of the activity and they interrelate with each other. "Running the game" is, therefore, not the whole thing at all. The other three parts—"preparing," "introducing," and "debriefing"—are integral parts of conducting a simulation/game.

PREPARING FOR THE SIMULATION/GAME

Obviously, you must be prepared if you want to conduct a simulation/game which requires flexibility and imagination. To prepare, read over the selected activity's purposes and rules carefully so that you know what to expect in general. You can then project how this simulation/game relates to your specific situation at school, recreation center, or home. If you feel that you need some practice before you play "for real," try out the simulation/game with a friend or small group of friends ahead of time. Even five minutes of "pilot" time will be of value if you feel a bit shaky. Sometimes you may simply wish to combine a pilot session with the real session by announcing that together the participants and you will practice the activity to get a feel for it before you actually begin.

Check to see that you have the necessary materials. You should have enough paper, pencils, and pennies for everyone to play comfortably, either individually or as a group. You can determine what you specifically need by checking the Materials item for the selected activity.

How to Conduct a Simulation/Game

    Make a proposed time schedule either on paper or in your head. In this way you will be sure not to use all the available time in introducing and running the simulation/game. You must allow adequate time to debrief the activity. Debriefing is not something added *after* the simulation/game. It is an *integral part* of the simulation/game.

    Arrange the space you have available so that you can play with ease. You may decide to look for additional or alternate space if the simulation/game requires participants to move around and you have a sizable group of people. Many activities fit in with just about any space you have, but it is wise to consider the use of space at all times because of the changing number of participants.

INTRODUCING THE SIMULATION/GAME

When you introduce the simulation/game, take care to be brief. If you say too much before play begins, then you may well rob the activity of its power. That is, the participants may lose the opportunity to discover the meaning of their actions for themselves. Keep in mind that you have time later in debriefing to help the players see the meaning and benefit of the entire activity. So, in your brief introduction relate the simulation/game to previous situations only in a broad sense. Give *only an overview* of the purpose and rules of the activity. You might say something like, "Here's something for us to try together. It reminds me of the things we did together last week. Let's get right into it and have some fun, and then we can talk about it later."

If you feel that the selected activity is a bit complicated for your players, then briefly explain that because any activity is complex, it is normal for some people to be perplexed in the beginning. Add that your role as leader will be to facilitate the playing and to help those players who are perplexed, or nervous, or uneasy. The key here is for you to be enthusiastic, serious, and decisive. This is a convincing cluster of qualities that is contagious.

RUNNING THE SIMULATION/GAME

Divide the participants, if necessary, into pairs, trios, or small groups. Distribute the necessary materials to start the simulation/game. Present the "scenario" of the situation to be simulated, if there is one. Explain the rules as they are needed, step-by-step. Do not give rules that will apply only later. Stay with the present, and announce rules for each situation as it arises to avoid overwhelming and confusing the players. In short, follow the step-by-step procedure given with each activity.

Announce any time limits. Your task is to keep the activity moving smoothly and within the time limits. Do not get bogged down with lots of explaining. Clarity will come as the simulation/game progresses.

If there is an extra player, ask him/her to be your Official Observer. Stress the point that this participant will play an important role later on when everyone begins to talk things over together. Ask the Official Observer to take some mental and written notes to help in reporting to the group in a short while.

Once the play gets going your function is to facilitate the action, explain needed new rules, and remain unobtrusive but helpful and observant. If you yourself are a participant in the play, enjoy yourself as you do double duty. Halt the action when the time runs out or when the players reach the point where they are ready for a debriefing discussion.

DEBRIEFING THE SIMULATION/GAME

Many simulation/game leaders claim that the debriefing part is the most important part of all. Here is the opportunity for the players to reflect on what they have done and to discover what it all means. Here is the opportunity for the players to find the answer to their legitimate questions, "What's this all about?" or "Why are we doing all of this?" or "What's the point of this?" Here is the opportunity to integrate the simulation/game with the player's other activities. Therefore, be sure to leave enough time for an adequate debriefing session. A poor debriefing session may yield a distorted picture of what the activity is about.

Sometimes it will simply be impossible to achieve all the purposes of a given activity in one session because there are too many discussion possibilities. Therefore, it may be necessary for you to take one of three paths. (1) Decide ahead of time which purposes you want to fulfill and plan your debriefing discussion accordingly. Ask those questions which will get at the points you wish to raise and discuss. (2) Start the debriefing session with a broad range of general questions in order to find out what aspects of the activity particularly interest your players. Continue the debriefing along the specific line the players favor. (3) Start with a broad range of questions and continue with a loose and general discussion by asking some varied questions relevant to the several issues raised by the activity. Plan on picking up any loose ends at a later time.

Within this debriefing strategy there are some sample questions for you to ask in addition to the ones you yourself will formulate for each specific activity. Obviously, there is no way here to list all the pertinent questions for each simulation/game in this book. These questions here are to get your debriefing discussion going and to guide it. No doubt you will not need to ask every planned question since many points will come up from the players even without your solicitation. Ask only those questions you want to and need to in order to keep the debriefing going.

Keep in mind when you debrief that your role in the recommended strategy is to be discussion facilitator and paraphraser. Do not "preach" to the players. Patience will pay off. Do not try to force out more from the players than they are willing to discuss because the forced points will probably not be meaningful anyway. Keep the extra points in mind and use other meeting times or activities to help you bring them out again to your players.

Shift into the debriefing session by simply saying something like "Now, let's talk about what happened so far."

(a) Begin the debriefing by encouraging the players to *describe what happened* so that all players will know what the others did. Let the players "ventilate." Without sufficient hard-fact ventilation, there will not be an adequate basis for making discoveries and drawing conclusions later on. This opening phase of the debriefing will loosen up the players and get them talking, as it is very easy to talk on this concrete, non-threatening level. Ask such questions as: What decisions did you make? What were the results of your decisions? What happened when the activity ended? How did you feel when you won (lost)? Were you able to predict another player's decisions after a while? What made you feel good during the action? What made you feel bad? What observations does the Official Observer have?

(b) *Analyze the meaning, purposes, or benefits* of the simulation/game. Ask such questions as: What do the results mean to you? What key ideas does this game teach us? What justifications do you have for the decisions you made? What did you learn about yourself and other players from playing?

(c) *Analyze the simulation/game design.* Compare and contrast the similarity of the action of the players with the events in other parts of their lives. Treat the specific features of the simulation/game scenario, rules, and sequence of events. Do not assume that the players realize what the various features of the simulation/game represent. Ask such questions as: In what ways is the picture presented by this activity similar to other parts of your life? In what ways is the picture presented by this activity different from other parts of your life? How do the various rules of this activity compare with the rules we follow in other parts of our life? What does the (part of game) represent in real life?

(d) *Plan future discussions, activities, and simulations/games* that can build upon the experience with this selected simulation/game. Try to launch new experiences that spring from this one. Ask such questions as: If we were to play this game again, what would you change? How can we change this activity to make it closer to what the real events are like? What key ideas from this simulation/game would you like to pursue in depth? Are there any related activities that you would like to do now?

(e) *Summarize, generalize, and conclude.* At various spots during the debriefing but especially at the end of a session there is great need for *tying points together*. Summarize the points made by the players. Encourage the players to generalize and draw conclusions, for here lies the educational benefit of the simulation/games. The generalizations and conclusions constitute the learning which arises from the activity. Do not assume that players will make generalizations and draw conclusions on their own without guidance. Request the players first to list some key ideas that have come forth during the discussion, then to offer some generalizations based on these ideas, and finally to draw some overall conclusions. Ask such questions as: What key ideas, in summary, have we talked about? What can you say in general based on these ideas? From all we've done and said, what conclusions can you draw from this simulation/game?

Once you have summarized, generalized, and drawn conclusions, launch into something new that you have explored earlier with the players. In this way you will bridge current activity with future activity while interest is still high.

With these guidelines for conducting a simulation/game you should be able to conduct an activity that will yield fun and educational benefit. In some of the simpler simulations/games you obviously will not need or use a complete discussion in each of these five debriefing sections. Use your judgment, but debrief you must for maximum educational benefit.

II
WHAT

> The instructor is relieved—at least during the period of the game—of his potentially disruptive role in the learning process, that of judge.
>
> PHILIP M. BURGESS AND JAMES A. ROBINSON

> The expansion of a child's mind can be a beautiful growth.
>
> SYLVIA ASHTON-WARNER

> Creating new games or modifying old ones is one way young people can explore things for themselves.
>
> HERBERT R. KOHL

4

Paper and Pencil Word Games

COULD BE

BENEFIT/PURPOSE: To enjoy a quick word game; to improve spelling; to increase vocabulary; to learn phonic patterns in words as an aid in reading and writing; to discover rhyming words and patterns.

MATERIALS: Paper and pencil

NUMBER OF PARTICIPANTS: One or more

Paper and Pencil Word Games

PROCEDURE:

1. Players start with 4 dashes on their papers.

2. One player chooses 2 letters and another player chooses 2 positions. Thus, if the first player chooses the letters E and R and the other chooses positions 2 and 4, the players each write on their sheets the following: __ E __ R.

3. Within a 2-minute time limit each player writes down as many 4-letter words as possible that fit this pattern. That is, what are the words that this pattern COULD BE?

4. Plural words formed by S or ES and verb endings of S, ES, ED, or ING are not allowed.

WINNER: The player who has the most words after playing a short series of COULD BE games is the winner.

EXAMPLE: Here is a youngster's COULD BE list from a 4-letter word game. Every one of the words below "could be."

Letters: A and R
Positions: 2 and 3
Time: 1½ minutes

Combination: __ A R __

1. hard
2. hare
3. bare
4. care
5. fare
6. bark
7. dart
8. cart
9. darn
10. tart
11. mart
12. dare
13. ware
14. barn
15. wart
16. pare

VARIATIONS:
1. Use 3-letter words for an easier game.
2. Use 5- or 6-letter words for a harder game.
3. Use 3 positions in a 5-letter word for an even harder game.
4. Change the letters and positions.
5. Reduce or increase the time limit.

NOTE/COMMENT: In the example you will notice that there are words that "could be" that the youngster didn't think of within the time limit. For example, hart, lark, and mark also fit the COULD BE pattern. This situation is common when players operate under a time limit. That's why it's good to share lists as suggested in the debriefing.

DEBRIEFING HINTS: After sharing the lists of words made up, check to see if everyone knows what the words mean; group the words that rhyme as one way of starting to form word patterns; use rhyming words to write short, comic verses; check the spellings of the words to see if they are correct.

ACROSS THE WORD

BENEFIT/PURPOSE: To enjoy a quick and simple word game; to learn new example of topics chosen; to improve spelling.

MATERIALS: Paper and pencil

NUMBER OF PARTICIPANTS: 2 or more; if more than 5 participate, then break up into small groups to facilitate comparison of items listed after each round.

PROCEDURE:

1. Players together decide on a topic such as automobiles, cities, inventors, animals, presidents, trees, or birds.

2. Each player writes this topic vertically, one letter to a line (using the singular form). For example:

> F
> L
> O
> W
> E
> R

3. Within a time limit of 2 minutes, each player writes the names of flowers that either begin with an F, L, O, W, E, or R or contain these letters.

4. No word may be listed more than once.

5. Each person tries to score as many points as possible according to the scoring system.

WINNER: The player who has the most points according to the scoring system given here is the winner after a sort series of games.

Scoring:
2 points for each example that begins with a
   letter of the topic
1 point for each example that contains
   a letter of the topic

EXAMPLE: Here is a list from a 9-year-old so intent on getting 2 points for each example that she forgot to list more 1-point examples of Plants That Grow.

		Points
<u>P</u>INE		2
<u>L</u>		0
<u>A</u>PPLE		2
BA<u>N</u>ANA		1
<u>T</u>		0
<u>S</u>QUASH		2
<u>T</u>OMATO		2
<u>H</u>OLLY		2
<u>A</u>FRICAN VIOLET		2
<u>T</u>		0
<u>G</u>RAPEFRUIT		2
<u>R</u>ADISH		2
<u>O</u>RANGE		2
<u>W</u>		0
		19

VARIATIONS:

1. Reduce the time limit to 1 minute for a harder game; increase the time limit to 3 or 4 minutes for an easier game.

2. Use topics of more than one word, such as Foreign Capital, American Author, Baseball Player, Plants That Grow, Girls' Names.

NOTE/COMMENT: It's fun to play a series of short ACROSS THE WORD games and to have players read off the examples they have listed. It gets players talking together and builds a good spirit for further play.

DEBRIEFING HINTS: Talk about the various examples listed. For example, for Plants That Grow talk about where oranges and

Paper and Pencil Word Games

grapefruit grow and just what an African violet is. Check to see if there are any developing patterns that players are unaware of on their lists; list examples that could have been used for 2 points and 1 point; check to see if spelling is correct for the various items.

WORD DETECTIVE

BENEFIT/PURPOSE: To enjoy a word game of detection; to practice and refine skills of deducing knowledge from given information; to learn new words.

33

Paper and Pencil Word Games

MATERIAL: Pencil and paper

NUMBER OF PARTICIPANTS: 2 individual players or 2 teams

PROCEDURE:

1. Each player writes down a secret 5-letter word that the other player is to detect. The secret word must have all 5 letters different.

2. Players alternate turns in asking each other 5-letter words. In responding to the other person a player tells only how many—but not which—letters of the asked word are also in his/her secret word. (See example.)

3. Whenever a player wishes, he/she may announce that on this turn he/she will be going for the word and not just for letters. The other player only responds Yes or No to the word. On this type of turn, he/she does not, if answer is No, give any clues about the number of similar letters between the asked word and the secret word. (See example.)

WINNER: The winner is the first player to detect the other's secret word.

EXAMPLE: Here is an annotated game that shows the rules of the game in action and also shows the process of deducing at each step. Keep in mind that a zero is a helpful response in detecting the secret word.

Turn	Word Asked	Response (how many letters in secret word)	Knowledge Deduced	Letters known at this point
1.	WROTE	1	You don't know which letter yet.	—
2.	WRECK	0	Cross out W,R, E,C,K, in the alphabet below; it's either T or O.	—

Paper and Pencil Word Games

Turn	Word Asked	Response (how many letters in secret word)	Knowledge Deduced	Letters known at this point
3.	WRITE (ask this to test the letter O)	2	You know it's I and T because it can't be the W, R, or E; cross out O from Turn #1.	I, T
4.	DINES	3	One is for the I; as it can't be the E, then it is 2 from D,N,S.	I, T
5.	DROWN	1	As it isn't the O, R, W, it's either the D or N; and you now know S is correct from Turn #4.	I, S, T
6.	STONE (to test the N you ask a word with T and S, which you know, and N.	3	N is correct; it's S,T,N, as O and E are already eliminated; you know 4 letters; cross out D from Turn #5.	I, N, S, T
7.	"Is your word STAIN?" (You ask this because what else beside A goes with I,N,S,T?	No	Didn't gain much.	I, N, S, T
8.	STAIN (just to be sure that A is in the word)	5	Yep, you've got all 5 letters.	A, I, N, S, T
9.	"Is your word SAINT?"	No	Wow, what can it be if it isn't STAIN or SAINT?	A, I, N, S, T
10.	"Is your word SATIN?"	Yes	You've got it; great detective!	SATIN

A B ~~C~~ ~~D~~ ~~E~~ F G H I J ~~K~~ L M N O P Q ~~R~~ S T U V ~~W~~ X Y Z

VARIATIONS:

1. For an easier game use a 4-letter word; for a harder game use a 6-letter word.

2. For a difficult game allow secret words that contain the same letter more than once, such as RIVER. The detective at the end of eliminating the incorrect letters of the alphabet will have only E, I, R, and V if the secret word is RIVER. It will be difficult to form these letters into a 5-letter word because the "detective" will now know which letter to double.

3. Allow double-letter words but require the players to tell which letters are doubled to make the game a bit easier.

NOTE/COMMENT: Young children can successfully play this game with some initial help to teach them how to deduce knowledge from the responses they receive. Also, children need help in strategically choosing words to ask to test out certain letters. After a few games with help, children can successfully detect the secret words. See a related game in this book, Target Practice, that involves numbers rather than letters.

DEBRIEFING HINTS: Talk about how the winner deduced the secret word; what was wisely or not wisely asked in each turn; what was deduced in each turn; if any errors in deduction were made through omission or commission; how players could have been better WORD DETECTIVES through better words asked and better deduction; check meaning of words to improve vocabulary.

HANGMAN

BENEFIT/PURPOSE: To enjoy a simple and fast secret-word game; to improve spelling; to practice skill of word completion from given hints.

36

Paper and Pencil Word Games

MATERIAL: Paper and pencil

NUMBER OF PARTICIPANTS: 2 or more

PROCEDURE:

1. One player, called the Hangman, chooses a secret word of 5 to 8 letters. (Sometimes it is helpful for the Hangman to write the word on a separate sheet of paper to refer to it as the game proceeds.)

2. The Hangman publicly draws a picture of a gallows on a sheet of paper and the appropriate number of dashes to indicate the size of the chosen word as follows (for a 6-letter word):

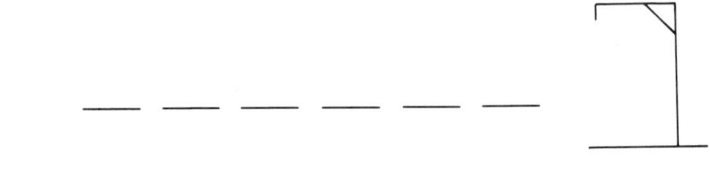

3. Each of the other players in turn asks a letter in trying to discover the secret word. The other players play together against the Hangman.

4. If the letter is in the secret word, then the Hangman writes that letter above the appropriate dash, as many times as it appears. If the letter is not in the secret word, then the Hangman adds a head to the gallows.

5. Play continues in this manner until the other players discover the secret word or until they are hanged by the Hangman. They are hanged when all parts of the person are added to the gallows in 8 misses in order as follows:

    a. Head
    b. Body
    c. Right leg and foot
    d. Left leg and foot
    e. Right arm and hand
    f. Left arm and hand
    g. Ears
    h. Face (eyes, nose, mouth)

37

Paper and Pencil Word Games

WINNER: The Hangman wins if he/she succeeds in hanging the other players (8 misses). The other players win if they succeed in discovering the secret word.

EXAMPLE: Here is an example of a game where the Hangman hanged the other players. It shows the full picture of the hanged person.

1. Guess O : __ __ __ __ __ __ __ __

2. Guess A : __ __ __ A __ __ __ __

3. Guess E : __ __ __ A __ __ __ __

4. Guess U : __ __ __ A __ __ __ __

5. Guess S : S __ __ A __ __ __ __

6. Guess W : S __ __ A __ __ __ __

7. Guess L : S __ __ A __ __ __ __

Paper and Pencil Word Games

8. Guess I : S _ _ _ A _ I _ _

9. Guess M : S _ _ _ A _ I _ _

10. Guess C : S _ _ _ A _ I _ _

11. Guess P : S _ _ _ A _ I _ _

The Hangman wins; the secret word is STRAIGHT.

VARIATIONS:

1. For a longer and easier game for the other players increase the number of steps before hanging by making the legs and feet, as well as the arms and hands and parts of the face, separate items.

2. For a harder game require that the Hangman write only one letter in its proper place each turn even though a guessed letter appears more than once in the secret word. Thus the other players may have to guess a letter more than once. For example, if the secret word is SLEEP and the guess is E, then the Hangman may write E on the third or fourth dash. The other players will not know that there are two E's and will have to guess E again. If they ask a letter twice but are incorrect on the second guess, it counts as a miss. If this variation is used, then increase the number of misses from 8 to 11 or 12.

3. For an easier game use short words (4 or 5 letters) and for a harder game allow a long word of any size (8 to 12 letters).

NOTE/COMMENT: This is an old-time favorite with youngsters, a game they can play over and over again. It is simple, yet exciting and challenging as the players watch the person develop in the picture drawn by the Hangman.

DEBRIEFING HINTS: Talk about the strategy used by the Hangman in choosing the secret word; the strategy used in guessing letters; what letters could have been chosen based on the pattern of the letters known at a given turn; spelling patterns as a clue for guessing letters to complete the secret word; the meaning of the secret word.

TYPES

BENEFIT/PURPOSE: To enjoy a perennially popular word game; to increase knowledge about the types of things chosen; to stretch our imagination; to improve spelling.

MATERIALS: Paper and pencil

NUMBER OF PARTICIPANTS: 2 or more; best with at least 3 players.

PROCEDURE:
1. Players choose a 5-letter word and 5 types of people, places, or things. They write the word and the 5 types on a 5 × 5 figure as follows (using the word SMITE and the types Cars, Foreign Cities, Flowers, Authors, and Boy's Name as example):

Paper and Pencil Word Games

	Cars	Foreign Cities	Flowers	Authors	Boy's Name
S					
M					
I					
T					
E					

2. Each player fills in his/her 25 squares in the following way: in the first column the names of cars that begin with S, M, I, T, and E; in the second column foreign cities that begin with S, M, I, T, and E; and so forth.

3. When playing with 3 or more players, there is a bonus for listing words not chosen by any other player. This bonus is for "stretching your imagination."

4. Players decide on a time limit. A 10- to 15-minute limit is suggested as a start.

5. The object is to get as many points as possible according to the scoring system when filling in the squares.

WINNER: In a 2-person game the player with the most squares filled is the winner. In a game with 3 or more players, the person with the most points according to the scoring system is the winner. It takes a little longer to score this way but it's well worth the effort.

Scoring:

3 points for each word no other player has used. 1 point for each word listed that someone else has, too. As the players announce their words when the time limit has expired, each player writes his/her score for each square in the lower right corner of the square. This will facilitate totaling the points earned.

41

Paper and Pencil Word Games

EXAMPLE: Here is an example of a game played with 2 other people. This player won. Can you think of words to fill in the empty squares?

	Cars	U.S. Cities	Boy's Name	Flowers	Famous Americans
I	Impala 1		Irwin 3	Iris 1	Washington Irving 3
T		Tucson 3	Thomas 1	Tulip 3	Truman 3
E	Electra 3	Easton 3	Elmer 3		Eisenhower 1
M	Mercury 1	Minneapolis 1	Myron 3		Madison 1
	5	7	10	4	8

Score = 34 points

VARIATIONS:

1. For an easier game use only 4 types across the top and/or a 4-letter word down the left side; for a harder game use 6 types and/or a 6-letter word.

2. For an easier game increase the time limit to 20 minutes; for a harder game reduce the time limit to 7 to 9 minutes.

3. For a harder game use a word with a double letter such as STOOP, HEEL, or even TEETH. This will challenge the players to think of twice as many types for certain letters.

4. Use other types such as Composer, Tools, Painters, U. S. Cities West of the Mississippi River, Countries, and Athletes.

NOTE/COMMENT: Use your imagination in playing Types not only in listing words no one else has but also in selecting types to list across the top. With imagination the number of games that can be played is endless.

DEBRIEFING HINTS: Talk about the various words listed for each type to acquaint players with, for example, the cars, foreign cities, and flowers listed; check to see that words are spelled correctly; comment on the imaginative words listed by the players.

FORMO

BENEFIT/PURPOSE: To enjoy a fast-paced word game; to learn new words; to learn to make an on-the-spot decision and build on it; to develop word facility by seeing words inside of longer words.

MATERIALS: Paper and pencil

NUMBER OF PARTICIPANTS: 2 to 5

PROCEDURE:

1. Each player draws his/her own gamesheet of 25 squares in which to write letters. (See example.)

2. Each player in rotation calls out any one letter of the alphabet.

3. Each player immediately writes the called letter in any square on the gamesheet, keeping in mind that the object is to form words. Words may be formed horizontally or vertically (but not diagonally), crossing each other as in a crossword puzzle.

4. Once a letter is written down it may not be moved to another position.

5. After all 25 squares are filled in by each person separately, players list the words formed on their gamesheets. Some letters may not be used in any word, some may be used in one word only, and others may be used in two or more words.

6. The object is to score as many points as possible according to the scoring system.

WINNER: The player who has the most points according to the scoring system is the winner.

    10 points for each 5-letter word.
    7 points for each 4-letter word.
    3 points for each 3-letter word.
    0 points for each 2-letter or 1-letter word.

a. 3-letter and 4-letter words contained within larger words count separately. That is, EAT in SEAT counts as a 3-letter word while SEAT itself counts as a 4-letter word.

b. Overlapping words also count separately. For example, in the row of 5 letters, AFARM, the words AFAR, FAR, FARM, and ARM all count separately.

c. Plurals formed by S and ES and verb endings of S, ES, ED, and ING do not count. Thus, EATS counts only as a 3-letter word.

EXAMPLE: Here is a winning gamesheet in a Formo game of 3 people.

M	E	R	E	E
A	F	A	R	M
N	E	G	R	O
O	S	E	A	T
R	E	S	T	S

VARIATIONS:

1. Change the order of players calling out letters.
2. Limit the number of vowels that can be called.
3. Prohibit the calling of certain letters.
4. Have a "doubles" game where pairs of players play against each other.

NOTE/COMMENT: If you play with very young players, then you might wish to count 2-letter words for 1 point each. Or, with young players you can supervise players to help them plan ahead and prepare for new words. It is especially helpful with young players to aid them in listing their words because they sometimes don't spot the words on their gamesheets.

DEBRIEFING HINTS: Talk about the words the players formed to be sure that the players understand them; check to see if players missed listing some words on their gamesheets; comment on how words can be found inside other words; comment that we can play with words and letters.

DOWN THE LINE

BENEFIT/PURPOSE: To enjoy a new word game; to learn new words; to improve spelling.

MATERIALS: Paper and pencil

NUMBER OF PARTICIPANTS: 2 or more

PROCEDURE:

1. Players choose a 4-letter word and write it horizontally above a square about 2" × 2 " divided into 16 smaller squares.

45

Paper and Pencil Word Games

Players number down to 4 along the left side. Thus, if they choose the word "SAME," the figure will look like this:

	S	A	M	E
1				
2				
3				
4				

2. Each player tries to fill in all his/her squares, in the following way. In the square S-1 the player writes a 4-letter word, a new 4-letter word that begins with S; in square S-2 a 4-letter word with S as the second letter; and so forth Down the Line with S. Players do the same for A, M, and E.

3. A player may use a word only once.

4. Plural words formed by S or ES and verb endings of S, ES, ED, and ING are not allowed.

WINNER: The player with the most squares filled in after 3 minutes is the winner. In case of a tie, the player who finished first is the winner.

EXAMPLE: This youngster won by filling in 15 of the 16 squares in 5 minutes. Can you think of a 4-letter word to complete the figure?

	S	T	O	P
1	spot	tree	oven	pool
2		stew	hope	open
3	mass	mate	hoop	tape
4	lass	flat	solo	step

VARIATIONS:

1. Increase the time limit to 4 to 8 minutes for an easier game; decrease the time limit to 1 or 2 minutes for a harder game.

2. Use a 5 × 5 figure with a 5-letter word across the top for a harder game.

3. For an easier game do not restrict the point words to the same size as the figure word. That is, if the figure word is SAME, allow 4-letter or longer words to be listed by the players.

4. Have players call out a word once they think of it. Everyone writes in that word in the appropriate square. The calling player thus captures this square. The winner is the player who has captured the most squares when all the squares are filled in or time has run out.

NOTE/COMMENT: This is a fast game that can be played many times over with a slight variation each time to maintain novelty.

DEBRIEFING HINTS: Talk about the words the players formed to be sure that everyone know them; check to see if words are spelled correctly; comment on the fun of playing with words.

BEEZE

BENEFIT/PURPOSE: To enjoy a new and engaging word game; to learn new words and thus increase our vocabulary; to improve spelling.

MATERIALS: Paper and pencil

NUMBER OF PLAYERS: 2 or more

Paper and Pencil Word Games

47 PROCEDURE;

1. One player picks 2 letters, and another player chooses the order of the letters. For example, if one player chooses R and O, another player may choose the order to be RO or OR.

2. Each player then draws three columns on his/her paper and heads them Back-to-Back, Breakthrough, and Bounced Around. (The name of this game derives from the fact that each column heading begins with the letter B; hence 3 "beeze.") Let's take as the 2 chosen letters R and O and keep them in that order. In the first column players write words that have R and O "back-to-back" anywhere in the word, as in rope, wrote, and pro. In the second column players wite words that have R and O in them in that order but where at least one other letter "breaks through" the pair as in ratio and furlong. In the third column players write words that have R and O in them but where the order has "bounced around" as in oral, cord, and cover. The gamesheet will look like this:

BACK-TO-BACK	BREAKTHROUGH	BOUNCED AROUND
RO	R O	OR

3. Words may be used only once.

4. Plural words formed by S or ES and verb endings of S, ES, ED, and ING are not allowed.

5. Players have 5 minutes to write as many words as they can to score as many points as possible according to the scoring system.

WINNER: The player who has the most points according to the scoring system is the winner.

Scoring:

5 points for every Back-to-Back word
3 points for every Breakthrough word
1 point for every Bounced Around word

EXAMPLE: Here is a young child's list after 8 minutes.

BACK-TO-BACK RO	BREAKTHROUGH RO	BOUNCED AROUND OR
Royal Root Roof Through Role Robot Robust Broth Robe Rock Rose Ross Ronald Froze Frolic Frosting	Orthodontist	Or For Older Folder Colder Order Forgery York
16 × 5 = 80	1 × 3 = 3	8 × 1 = 8

VARIATIONS:

1. Reduce the time limit to 3 minutes for a harder game; increase the time limit to 10 minutes for an easier game.

2. Use three letters for a very hard game.

3. For a hard game choose the same letter twice. Then there will be only Back-to-Back and Breakthrough words. For example, with "SS" you might have lass, miss, and assign as Back-to-Back words; you might have astonish, discuss, and squash as Breakthrough words.

4. Use strange combinations for a zany game.

Paper and Pencil Word Games

49

NOTE/COMMENT: Try a series of short Beeze game, some easy, some hard, for fun. Use your imagination in choosing letters and words.

DEBRIEFING HINTS: Talk about the words selected to check that all the players understand them; check to see that players have spelled the words correctly; comment on proper nouns, especially biographical and geographical words so that everyone knows the people and places named; check to see if players could have scored more points by placing words in a different column.

5

Penny-Moving Games

PENNY TIC TAC TOE

BENEFIT/PURPOSE: To enjoy a quick, more exciting game than the common paper and pencil Tic Tac Toe; to learn to plan ahead.

MATERIALS: Paper, pencil, and 6 pennies

NUMBER OF PARTICIPANTS: Two

PROCEDURE:
1. Players prepare a gamesheet by drawing a square about 6" × 6" divided into 9 smaller squares with each of the 9 squares

Penny-Moving Games

about 2" × 2". (See the reduced figure here; the squares are numbered only for ease in explaining and for remembering moves in a strategy.)

1	2	3
4	5	6
7	8	9

2. Each player has 3 pennies, and players decide who will be tails and who will be heads.

3. Players alternately place a penny on the gamesheet in any of the 9 squares. The object for each player is to get 3 of his/her pennies in a row either horizontally, vertically, or diagonally as in regular Tic Tac Toe.

4. If neither player has 3 in a row after all 6 pennies are down, then players move the pennies from square to square, any desired penny one square per turn, *sliding horizontally or vertically only,* in order to get 3 in a row as before.

WINNER: The first player to get 3 pennies in a row is the winner.

EXAMPLE: Here is how one gamesheet looked after each player had 4 turns. (H stands for heads; T stands for tails.) T's turn to move. What move would you make?

1 H	2 T	3 H
4	5 T	6
7	8 H	9 T

VARIATIONS:

1. The first player is not allowed to place a penny in the middle square on the first move.

2. In Step 4 of the procedure, players are allowed to slide their pennies horizontally, vertically, and diagonally but only along the *long* diagonals of the gamesheet that go from square 3 to 7 and from square 1 to 9.

3. In Step 4 of the procedure, players are allowed to slide their pennies horizontally, vertically, and diagonally along the long diagonals and also across the corners via the short diagonals, from squares 2 to 4, 2 to 6, 8 to 4, and 8 to 6.

4. In Step 4 of the procedure, players can move their pennies to any vacant square.

5. Play with 16 squares (a 4 × 4 gamesheet) and 4 pennies for each player.

NOTE/COMMENT: Penny Tic Tac Toe is a more complicated and hence exciting game than regular paper and pencil Tic Tac Toe. Both games are similar regarding control in that the player who controls the center square has the advantage. Nevertheless, there is no guarantee of a win in Penny Tic Tac Toe.

DEBRIEFING HINTS: Focus on the strategy each player used in placing pennies on the gamesheet initially and in sliding afterwards; stress the need to plan ahead via "If . . . then" thinking; to help develop strategies for playing better try some of the variations, especially Variation #2.

FOX AND GEESE

BENEFIT/PURPOSE: To enjoy a quick penny-moving game that involves no writing and no scoring; to practice planning ahead

Penny-Moving Games

with "If . . . then" thinking; to feel what it is like to be encircled and unable to move; to feel what it is like not to be able to stop the aggressor from achieving his/her goal.

MATERIALS: Paper, pencil, 5 pennies

NUMBER OF PARTICIPANTS: 2

PROCEDURE:

1. Players prepare an 8" × 8" playing sheet of 64 squares (about 1" × 1" each), coloring or shading in every other square, like a checkerboard. (See reduced playing sheet in the figures.)

2. Players decide who will be the Fox and who will be the Geese. The Fox is represented by one penny with the "head" of the coin showing. The Geese is represented by four pennies with the tail sides of the coins showing. The Geese places his/her four pennies on the shaded squares in the first row. The Fox places his/her penny on any shaded square in his first row. (See figure below.)

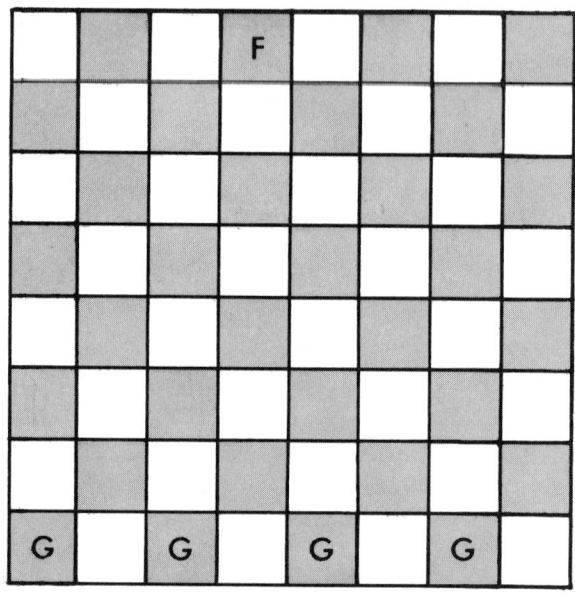

Penny-Moving Games

3. Player moves alternate according to these rules:

   a. The Fox moves as a king in checkers, from shaded square to shaded square one square at a time backward or forward. The Geese moves like a single checker, from shaded square to shaded square one square at a time *forwards only*.
   b. The Geese may move only a single penny in each turn—whichever penny is desired.
   c. Neither Fox nor Geese may capture or remove an opponent.
   d. Neither side may jump over any penny.
   e. Fox moves first.
   f. The object for the Fox is to reach the opposite side of the game sheet; the object for the Geese is to block the Fox and hem it in on all sides so that it can no longer move. (See the example for a middle-of-the-game position.)

Penny-Moving Games

56

WINNER: Fox wins if he/she reaches opposite side; Geese wins if he/she encircles the Fox.

EXAMPLE: Here is a middle-of-the-game position. The Fox and the Geese have each moved 4 times. It is now the Fox's turn to move again. If playing correctly, the Fox will win because there is no way for the Geese to block the Fox from moving forward through the Geese's line.

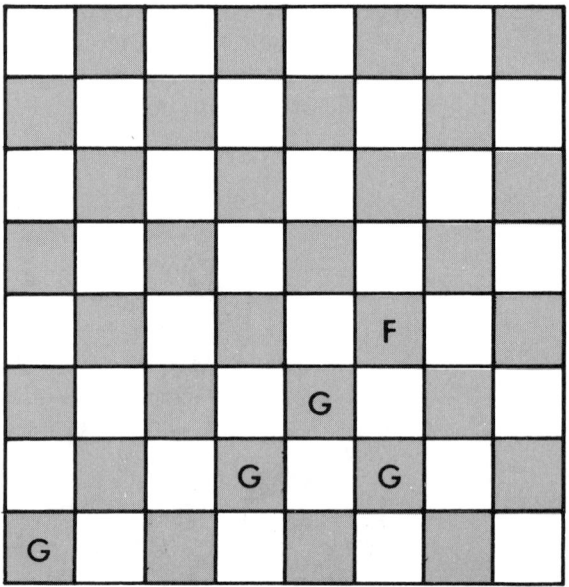

VARIATIONS:
1. The Geese moves first.
2. Set a time limit of 5 seconds for each move to speed up the game.
3. Switch roles after a few games.

NOTE/COMMENT: In this simple game of encirclement there is much opportunity for planning ahead. The Geese in order to encircle the Fox must try to keep a straight, horizontal line or at least a position that can easily be converted to one. The Fox must try to upset the Geese's line by continually attacking it to force a break-up of the line.

DEBRIEFING HINTS: Talk about what were the winning and losing moves; what strategy the winner used; what strategy the loser used; how the players can improve their games; how the Geese feels when constantly attacked by a predator "fox"; how the Fox feels when slowly and successfully encircled by the "geese"; which role, Fox or Geese, each player prefers.

SOLITAIRE AND DOUBLE SOLITAIRE

BENEFIT/PURPOSE: To enjoy a challenging game alone; to practice planning ahead; to compare your best game with another player in discovering a winning strategy.

MATERIALS: Paper, pencil, and 32 pennies for SOLITAIRE; 64 pennies for DOUBLE SOLITAIRE. (See example for illustration of gamesheet.)

NUMBER OF PARTICIPANTS: One for SOLITAIRE and two for DOUBLE SOLITAIRE.

PROCEDURE FOR SOLITAIRE:
1. Prepare a gamesheet as shown. If you have a big sheet of paper, then draw each of the 33 squares about 2" × 2". If you have only regular typing paper or notebook paper, smaller squares of 1" × 1" will suffice.

2. Place a penny on each square except the center one, 17.

3. Move by jumping one penny over the next, horizontally or vertically only (not diagonally), to an empty square beyond, as in checkers. Remove the jumped penny immediately. Thus, your first move can only be 5 to 17, or 19 to 17, or 29 to 17, or 15 to 17.

4. Your object is to remove all the pennies but one, and that one should be on square 17. Yes, it is possible.

PROCEDURE FOR DOUBLE SOLITAIRE:

1. Players prepare 2 gamesheets.
2. Players play as in Solitaire, but both players play simultaneously on their own gamesheets.

WINNER: In SOLITAIRE you win if you remove all the pennies but one and that one is on square 17. In DOUBLE SOLITAIRE the player with the fewer pennies left is the winner. If both players have the same number of pennies remaining, then the player who finished first is the winner.

EXAMPLE: Here is an end-game situation to work out as an introduction to playing SOLITAIRE. Put 6 pennies on squares 4, 5, 10, 16, 19 and 23. Your object is to make 5 moves (jumps) so that the last penny remaining will be on square 17. When you finish this, and it's not difficult, try a full game of SOLITAIRE with 32 pennies.

VARIATIONS:

1. Choose a different empty square to begin the game, and try to land the last penny on it.
2. Start with 2 empty squares, and try to end with a penny on each of these squares.
3. Set a time limit to keep the game going at a fairly fast pace.

NOTE/COMMENT: SOLITAIRE is one of the few penny-moving games you can play alone or easily convert into a two-person

Penny-Moving Games

	1	2	3		
	4	5	6		
7	8	9	10	11	12	13
14	15	16	17	18	19	20
21	22	23	24	25	26	27
	28	29	30		
	31	32	33		

game. It is possible to win in SOLITAIRE, but it takes much planning. If you can't find a winning set of moves, then write to me at Rutgers University in New Brunswick, N.J., for one set of winning moves (jumps).

DEBRIEFING HINTS: If you debrief yourself in SOLITAIRE, look for what you can do to improve your game; what strategy you can develop to land on square 17 at the end; how you can improve your score with an observer advising you. If you play DOUBLE SOLITAIRE, talk about the moves that led to different results; look for good tips from the other player.

PENNY ROYAL

Penny-Moving Games

BENEFIT/PURPOSE: To enjoy a new, fast, and yet challenging simple game; to practice planning ahead with "If . . ., then" thinking.

MATERIALS: 10 pennies (See Note/Comment section.)

NUMBER OF PARTICIPANTS: 2

PROCEDURE:

1. Players arrange the ten pennies—all heads up—in a "bowling pin" pattern as follows (numbered only for ease in explaining and for remembering moves in a strategy):

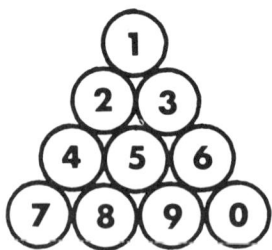

2. Players alternately move pennies from one position to another according to these 4 simple rules:

   a. You must be able to slide a penny into the open without disturbing any other penny.
   b. Once the penny is in the open, turn it over "tails up" and slide it back into any position so that it legally *nestles up* against 2 or more pennies, not *between* 2 pennies.

These are legal nestles for pennies 3 and 4:

61

Penny-Moving Games

This is an illegal nestle for penny 3:

c. You can only move "heads up" pennies.
d. You cannot slide a penny back into the position it came from.

3. The object is to be able to move a penny and to prevent the other player from doing so.

WINNER: The player who moves last is the winner.

EXAMPLE: Here is a game in which the first player wins. Set up 10 pennies and try out this game to see how it works (see Note/Comment section).

Player #1—Slides 1 to nestle against 8, 9.
Player #2—Slides 0 to nestle against 7, 8, 1.
Player #1—Slides 6 to nestle against 4, 7.
Player #2—Slides 3 to nestle against 7, 0
Player #1—Slides 2 to nestle against 6, 7, 3
Player #2—Slides 9 to nestle against 4, 5
Player #1—Slides 5 to nestle against 8, 1.
Player #2—Cannot move and thus loses.

This is the last position made by Player #1 forcing Player #2 to lose because no heads up penny (4, 7, or 8) can legally move.

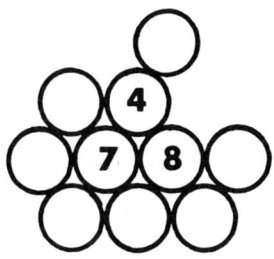

VARIATION: For a longer game play with 15 pennies arranged in a similar pattern but with 5 rows of pennies rather than 4.

NOTE/COMMENT: For ease in keeping track of the pennies as you play or try out the game described in the Example section, it is most helpful to have 10 pennies, each with a different date. From a stack of pennies select 10 with different last digits in the date. This will help because the pennies move around into unique positions.

DEBRIEFING HINTS: This is a "lighthearted" game not intended for heavy analysis in the debriefing, yet it is certainly possible to talk about the key moves made by the winner; what alternative moves the loser had; how to improve the moves made through better "If . . ., then" thinking as players plan ahead.

TAC TIX

BENEFIT/PURPOSE: To enjoy an intriguing take-away game; to practice planning ahead with "If . . ., then" thinking.

MATERIALS: 16 pennies

NUMBER OF PARTICIPANTS: 2

PROCEDURE:
   1. Players arrange 16 pennies in 4 rows of 4 each as follows (numbered only for ease in explaining and for remembering moves in a strategy):
   2. Players alternately take away pennies according to these two simple rules:

Penny-Moving Games

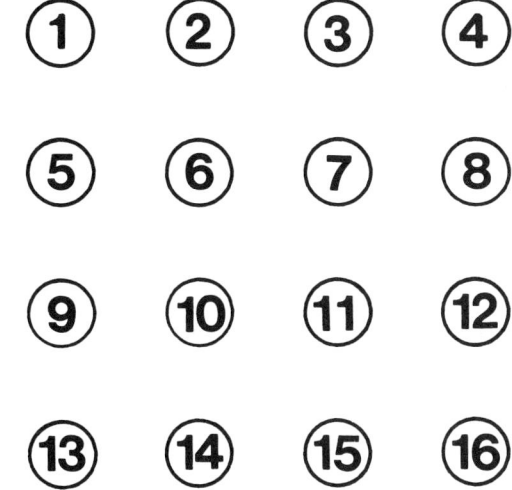

a. Take as many and whichever pennies you wish from any single column or row (but not a diagonal).
b. Pennies taken must be adjoining, no empty spaces between them. For example, assume that the first player took penny 3 in the top horizontal row. If you also wish to take pennies from that top row, then you cannot take pennies 1, 2, and 4 together in one turn because there is an empty space between 2 and 4. You may take only penny 1, or 1 and 2, or 2, or 4. Of course, you may take from any other column or row.

3. Players try *not* to take the last penny.

WINNER: The winner is the player who forces the other player to take the last penny. In other words, the player who takes the last penny is the loser.

EXAMPLE: Here is a problem situation to solve as suggested by the designer of the game, Piet Hein of Copenhagen, Denmark. Working on this situation will serve as an introduction to or summary of the rules as you proceed. Find a move that will guarantee you a win. (Two such moves are possible.)

Penny-Moving Games

VARIATIONS:
1. For a longer and more complex game use a 5 × 5 or 6 × 6 arrangement of pennies.
2. For a simple game try a 3 × 3 arrangement of 9 pennies. With this arrangement there is a winning strategy the first player can utilize whereas at this point there is no known strategy for the bigger arrangements using 16, 25, or 36 pennies.
3. Play with a 4 × 4 arrangement where the 4 corner pennies (1, 4, 13, 16) are missing.

NOTE/COMMENT: This modern classic game is more complex than it might seem. The complexity arises from the high number of possible moves and intersecting sets of pennies. Play TAC TIX and see.

DEBRIEFING HINTS: Talk about the strategy used by the winner; the key moves and the losing moves of the game; the moves the players should have made had they planned ahead well; how it feels to be stuck with the last penny.

Penny-Moving Games

COUNTDOWN

BENEFIT/PURPOSE: To enjoy a simple but challenging take-away game; to practice adding and subtracting; to practice planning ahead with "If . . ., then" thinking.

MATERIALS: 19 to 30 pennies

NUMBER OF PARTICIPANTS: 2 or 3

PROCEDURE:
1. Players agree on amount of pennies to be in the starting pile, from 19 to 30.
2. Players alternately remove pennies from the pile.
3. Players must take 1 or 2 or 3, whichever they choose, on each move. They may change the amount they take each time or take the same amount as before. But they must take at least one penny each turn.
4. Each player tries to take the last penny either by itself or together with 1 or 2 other pennies.

WINNER: The player who takes the last penny by itself or together with 1 or 2 other pennies is the winner.

EXAMPLE: Here's a complete 2-player game played with 19 pennies. Carole won this game. Jerry could have won but made an error on his third move. Can you figure out what Jerry's strategic error is?

1.	Carol	removes 2,	leaving 17
	Jerry	removes 1,	leaving 16
2.	Carol	removes 1,	leaving 15
	Jerry	removes 3,	leaving 12

3.	Carol	removes 1,	leaving 11
	Jerry	removes 2,	leaving 9
4.	Carol	removes 1,	leaving 8
	Jerry	removes 3,	leaving 5
5.	Carol	removes 1,	leaving 4
	Jerry	removes 1,	leaving 3
6.	Carol	removes 3	and wins.

VARIATIONS:
 1. Add more pennies to the starting pile.
 2. Change the number of pennies that may be taken each time. For example, each player can take 1 or 2 or 3 or 4 pennies.
 3. Assign different amounts allowable to different players.
 4. Play that the winner in a 2-person game is the one who *does not* take the last penny.

NOTE/COMMENT: This is the simplest of take-away games, yet challenging enough to keep youngsters and adults actively searching for a way to win consistently. The older the players the better it is to have a big pile of pennies to keep them on their mental toes.

DEBRIEFING HINTS: Talk about the moves the winner made that were crucial in winning; the critical moves made by the loser; what is a strategy for always winning; how to win even with game variations; how to keep track of the amount of pennies removed during the game.

NIM

BENEFIT/PURPOSE: To enjoy a fast game; to learn the "grandfather" of the penny take-away games; to learn the powers of 2; to learn to work in the base 2 in math; to learn about computer math (binary math).

Penny-Moving Games

67

MATERIALS: 15 to 30 pennies

NUMBER OF PARTICIPANTS: 2

PROCEDURE:

1. To start a simple, basic game players place 15 pennies in three rows of 3, 5, and 7 pennies like this:

• • •

• • • • •

• • • • • • •

2. Players move alternately; either can go first.
3. Each player may remove as many pennies as he/she wishes—even the whole row—but from only one row each turn.
4. Player must take at least one penny each turn.
5. The object is to take the last penny.

WINNER: The player who removes the last penny (separately or together with others in the same row) is the winner.

EXAMPLE:

1. Here is an example of a complete game of the basic 3-5-7 formation. It will help you to set up 15 pennies and remove them as you read the moves that follow.

• • •

• • • • •

• • • • • • •

1. Joanna removes 2 from top row, leaving: 1 - 5 - 7
2. David removes 3 from middle row, leaving: 1 - 2 - 7
3. Joanna removes 2 from bottom row, leaving: 1 - 2 - 5
4. David removes 1 from bottom row, leaving: 1 - 2 - 4

5. Joanna removes 1 from middle row, leaving: 1 - 1 - 4
6. David removes 4 from bottom row, leaving: 1 - 1
7. Joanna removes 1 from top row, leaving: 1
8. David removes 1 from middle row and wins.

2. Here is an end-game position. It's your move. If you make the correct move, you can guarantee yourself a win. Work on this to help you get familiar with NIM.

•

• •

• •

VARIATIONS:

1. Have 4 or more rows and have a different number of pennies in each row. That is, add pennies and rows. It is possible to play with *any number of rows and any number of pennies in any row.*

2. Set up a particular formation such as "Bowling Nim" with 4 or 5 rows. For example, "Bowling Nim" may look like this with either 10 or 15 pennies:

3. Allow a player *if he/she wishes* to remove pennies from a row and then divide that row into two separate rows. For example: In the case of 3 rows of 2 - 5 - 7, remove 2 from the bottom row of 7 and divide the 5 remaining pennies into rows of 2 and 3 so that you leave 4 rows of 2 - 5 - 2 - 3.

4. Play "Checkerboard NIM." Place 8 heads and 8 tails on a gamesheet drawn like a checkerboard. (See Fox and Geese

Penny-Moving Games

gamesheet) Each player has 8 pennies on his/her side, in either the last or the next to last row, with one penny in each column. Thus, there will be one "tail" penny and one "head" penny in each column facing each other. Player plays alternately, advancing any of his/her 8 pennies toward the opponent's penny as many spaces as desired to close the gap between pennies. No jumping, no passing the opposing penny, only closing the gap. Thus, at most there will be only 6 spaces between 2 opposing pennies at the start of the game. When 2 pennies in a column meet, neither can move any more as there are no empty spaces between them. The last player to move a penny wins.

5. Play "Checkerboard NIM" as above but allow a player to move backward as well as forward if desired. Still no jumping. First person unable to move loses.

6. Play regular NIM, but this time the person who takes the last penny loses. That is, the person who forces the other to take the last penny wins.

NOTE/COMMENT: NIM is one of the oldest math games in the world. It is a classic of classics. NIM was a hit in the movie "Last Year in Marienbad." Theaters gave out books of matches to the audience that described the rules of the game on the inside covers. Nim is also used in many of the new math curriculums to teach the base 2. It has never failed me in challenging players—I often take on a group of ten or more at a time—to beat me. I invariably win and they invariably try to figure out how to beat me. So they start asking questions. I stipulate that I'll answer questions put to me only in Yes/No form. I answer all questions honestly and as often as they are asked. Finally, the participants request me to tell them how to win. I tell them that I will explain it only if they want me to. They answer "Yes, we want you to explain to us how to win." What a great teaching situation. By popular demand I proceed without any math jargon to explain only "how to win." It is always amazing how everyone—yes, everyone—learns the powers of 2 and binary math without realizing it. Even those people with

Penny-Moving Games

a block against "math" or computers learn the powers of 2, how to use the powers of 2, and computer math. It's fantastic! (See the Appendix for the explanation.)

DEBRIEFING HINTS: The most significant part of the debriefing is talking about the winning strategy. Talk about the players' moves that helped them win, what they can do to improve, how they can plan ahead with "If . . ., then" thinking.

If you know the explanation for strategically playing NIM (see "How to Win at Nim" in the Appendix), then teach the other players *only* if they request you to do so. Especially for younger players, explain only Method #2, as this is the one they can and will use when they play. Use actual penny positions of NIM as you explain. Talk about any situations where we use binary math in our daily lives, especially computers.

Definitely do not impose an explanation on players who do not want one. They may wish to figure it out themselves or even play as if there is no explanation so that everyone has an equal chance to win and lose.

So, if you're interested in the explanation of NIM see the Appendix. If not, have a good time playing NIM without it.

6

Paper and Pencil Line and Number Games

SQUARES

BENEFIT/PURPOSE: To enjoy a traditionally popular game of enclosing space; to learn to plan ahead; to practice counting.

MATERIALS: Paper and pencil

NUMBER OF PARTICIPANTS: 2 or 3

Paper and Pencil Line and Number Games

PROCEDURE:

1. Players prepare a gamesheet with 81 dots in 9 × 9 arrangement as follows:

2. Players alternately draw a line—horizontal or vertical only—connecting two adjacent dots not already connected.

3. Players try to complete squares. Each time a player completes a square by drawing the fourth and final side, he/she writes an identifying initial or color in the square. Then the player must take another turn. The player continues until he/she no longer completes a square. If a line completes two squares at the same time, the player still gets only one more turn to draw one further line.

A player may refuse to complete a square even if it is available with 3 completed sides. The player may choose to draw a line elsewhere on the gamesheet. (A player would do so in a situation that would eventually force another player to yield him/her many other squares, especially at the end of the game.)

WINNER: The player with the most completed squares when the figure is completed is the winner.

73

Paper and Pencil Line and Number Games

EXAMPLE: The figure below shows a game underway with S beating R by 2 to 1 at this point. It is R's turn. If R draws one line in the middle of the rectangle in the upper right area, then R will gain 2 more squares plus another turn. If R draws one line anywhere in the tunnel in the bottom right corner, then S can win 5 squares on S's next turn. Near the end of the game it might be wise in such a situation for R to draw the third side of the square in the upper left corner and thus tempt S to complete several squares. Then S would be forced to yield five squares—a net gain for R.

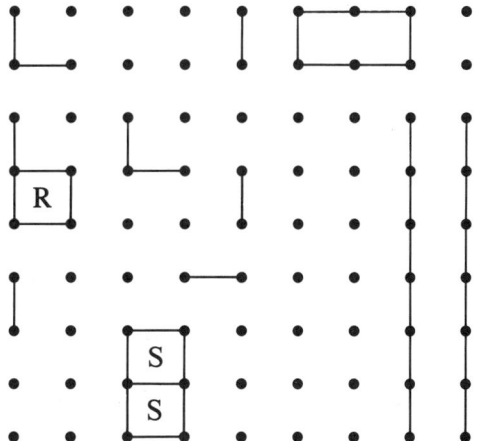

VARIATIONS:
1. For a shorter game prepare a smaller gamesheet figure of 6 × 6 or 7 × 7.
2. For a longer game prepare a larger gamesheet figure of 10 × 10 or 11 × 11.
3. Require that a player complete a square if it is available with 3 sides already drawn.

NOTE/COMMENT: This game is perennially popular because of its simplicity and challenge. A good player must plan ahead. The game offers a new pattern each re-play, and thus we can always come back to SQUARES for an enjoyable and strategically satisfying game. For a similar game in some respects see SLITHER in this book.

DEBRIEFING HINTS: Talk about the successful strategy used by the winner: what traps were set, avoided, and fallen into by the players; what were significant moves in the game and the alternatives available at the time; how to play ahead a few moves at a time.

TARGET PRACTICE

BENEFIT/PURPOSE: To enjoy a challenging "detective" type game; to practice and refine the skills of deducing knowledge from clues.

MATERIALS: Pencil and paper

NUMBER OF PARTICIPANTS: 2 individual players or 2 teams

PROCEDURE:
1. Each player secretly selects a 3-digit number—each digit a different numeral from 0 to 9.
2. Players write their numbers on their sheets of paper so they can refer to them.
3. Alternately each player asks the other player a 3-digit number in trying to discover the other player's secret number. The player asked responds with MISS, HIT, or BULLSEYE. A MISS means that no numeral asked is in the secret number. A HIT means that a numeral asked is in the secret number but in a different position. A BULLSEYE means that a numeral asked is in

Paper and Pencil Line and Number Games

the secret number and also in the correct position. The player must tell how many HITS and BULLSEYES if there are some. Thus, the player may, for example, answer 1 HIT or 2 HITS and a BULLSEYE, depending on the secret number. (There are 9 possible combinations of MISS, HIT, and BULLSEYE.)

WINNER: The first player to score 3 BULLSEYES (that is, to detect the other player's secret number) is the winner.

EXAMPLE: Below is an annotated game that shows the process of deducing at each step. Keep in mind that a MISS is a helpful response in deducing the secret number.

Paper and Pencil Line and Number Games

Turn	Number Asked	Score	Knowledge Deduced
1.	760	1 Bullseye	There's a 7, 6, or 0 in the secret number in that position.
2.	743	Miss	The number is __ 6 __ or __ 0; 7, 4, and 3 aren't in the number.
3.	869	1 Bullseye and 1 Hit	Looks like __ 6 __, but it could be the 8 or 9 giving the Bullseye and the other the Hit.
4.	840	2 Bullseyes	Must be 8 __ 0 since we know 4 is not in the number. Also, the Hit in Turn #3 above must be from the 9 as it can't be the __ 6 __ referring to Turn #1. Therefore, the number must be 8 9 0.
5.	890	3 Bullseyes	We were right! It is 890.

VARIATIONS:
 1. Use a 4-digit number for a harder game.
 2. Allow numerals to be used twice or three times for a very hard game.
 3. For an easier game play with teams to have help in deducing.

NOTE/COMMENT: Young children, 8 and 9, can successfully play this game with some initial help to teach them how to deduce knowledge from the responses they receive. Also, children need help in strategically choosing the number to ask to test out certain possibilities. After a few short games with help, children can do a powerful job of deductively detecting the secret number via good TARGET PRACTICE. See a related game in this book, WORD DETECTIVE.

DEBRIEFING HINTS: Talk about how the winner deduced the secret number; what was deduced in each turn; if any errors in deduction were made through omission or commission; why numbers asked were selected; if numbers asked were optimum numbers; how players could have improved their TARGET PRACTICE through better numbers asked and better deductions.

SIM

BENEFIT/PURPOSE: To enjoy a fast, challenging game of line-drawing; to practice recognizing triangles and other polygons.

MATERIAL: Paper and 2 pencils (preferably with different-color leads).

NUMBER OF PARTICIPANTS: 2

PROCEDURE:

1. Players place 6 dots on a sheet of paper to represent the 6 outside points of a hexagon as follows:

•

• •

• •

•

2. Alternately players draw lines from one dot to another. (There are 15 possible lines with these 6 dots.) Each player draws a line with a different color. (If only regular lead pencils are available, then one player draws a dashed line to separate the lines of the two players.)

3. Players try not to form triangles of their own color. Only triangles whose own 3 end points are among the 6 starting dots count.

WINNER: The player who forces the other to form a triangle of the other's own color wins. In other words, the player who forms a triangle of his/her own color loses. Keep in mind that only certain triangles count—those whose 3 end dots are from the 6 original dots.

78

**Paper and Pencil
Line and Number
Games**

EXAMPLE: Here is an example of a game in progress that has only one line left of the 15 possible ones. Each player has drawn 7 lines. Whoever goes next loses.

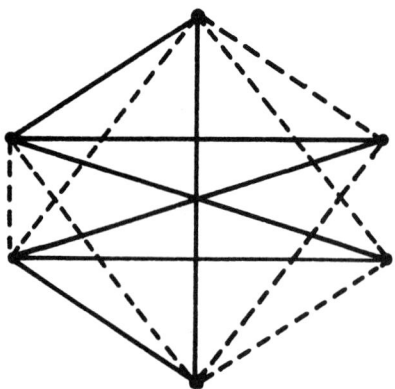

Here is a second example of a game in progress where dashed line went first. Dashed and solid have each drawn 6 lines, and it is now Dashed's turn. Dashed loses no matter which line of the 3 possible ones left is drawn. How did Dashed get into this mess? Even if it were Solid's turn, Dashed will lose on its next move because Solid does have one good move left.

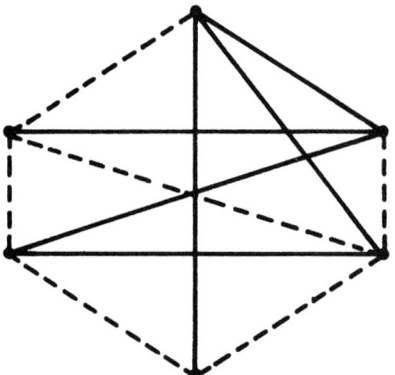

VARIATIONS:

1. For a longer and more complex game start with 7 or 8 dots, the vertices of a heptagon or octagon.

2. For a short and simpler game start with 5 dots, the vertices of a pentagon.

NOTE/COMMENT: SIM, like other games, is more sophisticated than it initially appears to be. SIM involves careful observation of the entier playing area, especially with larger polygons, lest you inadvertently form a triangle.

DEBRIEFING HINTS: Talk about critical lines drawn by the winner; the key losing lines drawn by the loser; the ease or difficulty in keeping track of the triangles formed with each line after the first few have been drawn; how many triangles have been drawn altogether, using only the 6 original dots as vertices.

SPROUTS

BENEFIT/PURPOSE: To enjoy a simple but mathematically intriguing line-drawing game; to learn something about the field of mathematics called Topology (Topology is the branch of geometry that studies those properties of figures or solid bodies which remain invariant under all continuous distortion.); to practice planning ahead with "If . . ., then" thinking.

MATERIALS: Paper and pencil

NUMBER OF PARTICIPANTS: 2; with more than 2 it is best played by dividing the group into pairs playing against one another. In each pair the player who wins 2 out of 3 games is declared the winner. Winners play each other, as in a tennis tournament, until a champion emerges.

Paper and Pencil Line and Number Games

PROCEDURE:

1. Players randomly place 5 dots, called spots, on a sheet of paper with adequate space between them to avoid congestion later on. Here is a typical beginning arrangement:

2. Players alternately draw a smooth arc joining one spot to another or to itself. Then the player places a new spot anywhere on the line of the arc. Thus, if we have only two spots, A and B, the first player may make one of these five moves:

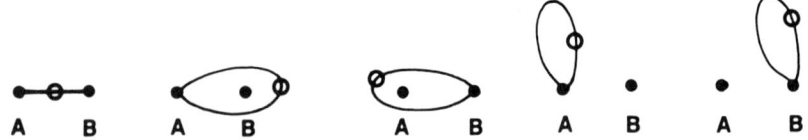

3. Play proceeds in this manner according to two further simple rules:

   a. An arc may have any shape, but it may not cross itself, or pass through any other line, or pass through a spot.
   b. No spot may have more than 3 arcs coming out of it. (When a spot is added to an arc it divides the arc into 2 parts; thus that spot already has two arcs coming out from it. Only one more arc may leave that spot.)

Here are examples of valid and invalid moves that will clarify these 2 rules. The solid spots are the original 5; the small open ones are spots added during play; they are drawn differently here for explanation purposes only.

5 LEGAL MOVES

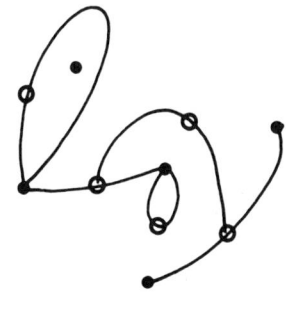

2 ILLEGAL MOVES
(dashed lines---)

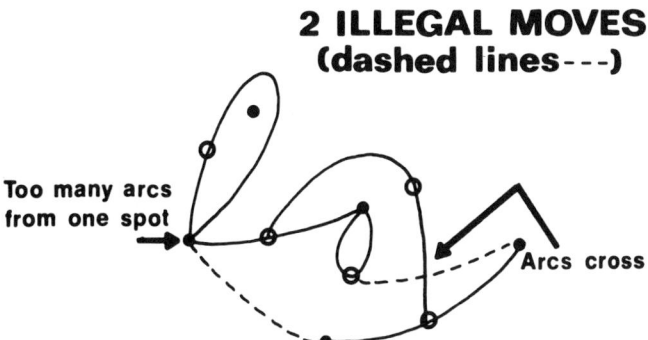

Too many arcs from one spot

Arcs cross

4. Players try to prevent each other from being able to make legal moves.

WINNER: The player who makes the last legal move is the winner.

EXAMPLE: Here is a game with 5 dots. Can you find any further moves?

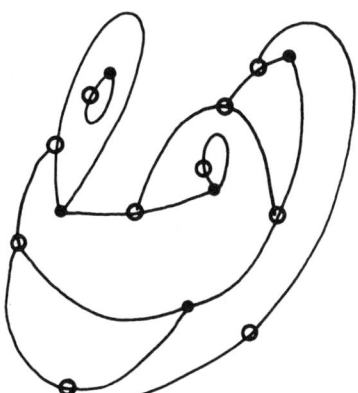

VARIATIONS:

1. For a longer and more complex game begin with 6 to 8 spots, or even 10.

2. For a shorter and easier game begin with 2 to 4 spots.

3. Play that the winner is the first player not able to make a legal move. In other words, the player who makes the last legal move is the loser.

NOTE/COMMENT: The name SPROUTS derives from the fact that during play strange and beautiful designs sprout from the original spots. Very young children can learn to play SPROUTS successfully because of its simplicity.

DEBRIEFING HINTS: Talk about the winner's strategy; about the loser's key moves; the number of possible moves in any game of SPROUTS (see the following discussion); the alternative moves available to the players at a given turn; how each closed arc divides space into an outside and an inside region; how a player could improve his/her playing by planning ahead with "If . . ., then" thinking; the amazing designs that the players create by playing.

Every spot has 3 "lives" to it. A spot is "dead" once it has 3 arcs coming out from it. Thus, a 5-spot game begins with 15 possible "lives" because each spot may have 3 arcs coming out from it. The first player uses up 2 of those lives, but adds 1 life when he/she adds a new spot to the arc just drawn. Therefore, after the first turn there are 15-2+1=14 lives left in the game. After the second move there are 13 lives left and so on. After the 14th move there is only 1 life left. Thus the game must end, as each move requires 2 lives.

In this way, a 5-spot game has a maximum of 14 moves, a 6-spot game a maximum of 17 moves, and a 7-spot game a maximum of 20 moves. In other words, each game has one move less than 3 times the original spots.

Also, a 5-spot game must have at least 10 moves; a 6-spot game at least 12 moves, and a 7-spot game at least 14 moves.

83

NUMERATE

Paper and Pencil Line and Number Games

BENEFIT/PURPOSE: To enjoy a fast-paced counting game; to learn to plan ahead; to practice counting.

MATERIALS: Paper and pencil

NUMBER OF PARTICIPANTS: 2 to 4

PROCEDURE:

1. Players prepare a 25-box figure about 2" × 2", with each box measuring ½" × ½", as shown.

2. Alternately, players begin counting and writing numbers in the figure. The first person writes the number 1 in any box. From then on, the players in turn write the next number in the figure according to these 2 simple rules:

   a. The new number must be in the same row or column (not diagonal) as the preceding number.
   b. The new number may be next to the preceding number or separated from the preceding number by empty boxes only. That is, a previously written number already in the figure may not stand between the new number and the one immediately preceding it.

3				
4		5		
2			1	

Paper and Pencil Line and Number Games

Thus, in the figure below, 5 can be written only in the same row as 4, as it cannot fit any longer in the same column with 4 (the 2 would stand between the 4 and the 5, which is not allowed).

3. The object is to prevent the other player from being able to write the next number.

WINNER: The last person to write a number successfully is the winner. If there are a series of games, the winner is the one who wins the most games.

EXAMPLE: Note in this sample game between two players that the "odd" player would have lost had she written 9 just to the left of 8. This is so because the "even" player would have written 10 in the lower left-hand corner, leaving the "odd" player no place to write 11, and thus "even" would have won. The "odd" player wins with 17, as there is no space for the "even" player to write 18.

14	13	9		
15	17	16	1	
3	12	11	2	
4		10	6	5
		8	7	

VARIATIONS:

1. Use a 16-box figure for a shorter game and a 36-box figure for a longer game.

Paper and Pencil Line and Number Games

2. Count by 2, 3, 4, or whatever to review counting by these numbers. If a player writes the wrong number, the other player automatically wins.

3. Keep score and count points in a series of games. The winner for each game gets the number of points equal to the last number he/she successfully wrote. After a series of games the winner is the player with the highest point total.

4. Keep score and count points. Furthermore, with each new game *continue counting* so that there is an increasingly higher winning score for each game. That is, the winning stake gets higher and higher. As above, the winner is the player with the highest point total after a series of games.

NOTE/COMMENT: Plan ahead; it's a challenge. It's not as easy as you think.

DEBRIEFING HINTS: Talk about the moves made; about the traps set and traps avoided; how the winner planned ahead to win; the correct numbers when you count by 2, 3, 4, 6, or whatever; the mounting pressure when you keep score and total points, continuing the counting from one game to the next to have higher and higher stakes.

SLITHER

BENEFIT/PURPOSE: To enjoy a recent, quick, but challenging game of enclosing space; to learn to plan ahead.

MATERIALS: Paper and pencil

NUMBER OF PARTICIPANTS: 2

Paper and Pencil Line and Number Games

86 PROCEDURE:

1. Players prepare a gamesheet with 30 dots in a 5 × 6 arrangement as follows:

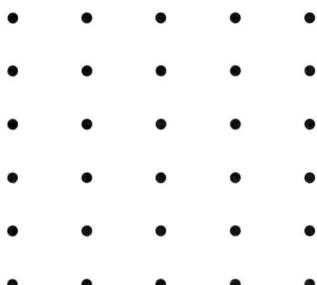

2. Players alternately draw a line—horizontal or vertical only—from one dot to another.

3. After the first line is drawn anywhere on the figure, each player must in turn extend the line one segment, from either end. That is, the new segments must form a continuous line as they are added to previous segments, from either end of the existing line.

4. The object is to avoid closing the line in such a way as to form a closed loop anywhere along the path.

WINNER: The player who *does not* close the path is the winner.

EXAMPLE: In the sample game, the next player obviously should not move on the left. If the next player instead extends the end on the right horizontally to the left rather than downwards or to the right, he/she will win on the next move.

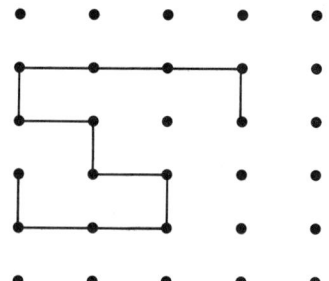

VARIATIONS:

1. For a longer, more complex game start with a larger gamesheet figure of 6 × 6 or 7 × 6 dots.

2. For a less exciting game, agree that the winner is the one who does close the path.

NOTE/COMMENT: This seemingly easy game offers many challenges. It bears only an apparent resemblance to the popular game of Squares also included in this book.

DEBRIEFING HINTS: Talk about which moves were critical ones; what the alternatives were at a given turn in the game; how to plan ahead a few moves at a time; what strategy the winner used; what the loser can do to plan ahead better to win.

S-O-S

BENEFIT/PURPOSE: To enjoy a game from Iran; to learn to plan ahead with "If . . ., then" thinking; to realize that a person has difficulty seeing every opportunity before him.

MATERIALS: Paper and 2 or 3 pencils (a pencil of a different color for each player, if possible)

NUMBER OF PARTICIPANTS: 2 or 3

PROCEDURE:

1. Players draw a lattice of 5 × 5 lines as follows:

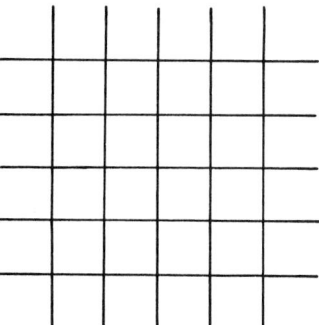

Paper and Pencil Line and Number Games

2. If there are 2 players, they play alternately. If there are 3 players, they play in rotation.

3. Each player writes either an S or an O in any cell of the lattice. The object for each player is to form an SOS, that is, to create a line of any 3 letters in a straight line (as in Tick-Tack-Toe) to spell the emergency call of S-O-S.

4. Once a player creates and SOS, he/she draws a line through it, marks a tally under his/her name on the gamesheet (to keep score), and then moves again. The player may then write either an S or an O in any cell. If two lines are formed with one move, the player can claim credit for both, but will still get only one more turn.

5. Any letter written in the lattice may be used as often as possible to create a new line of SOS. A line of SOS may be created horizontally, vertically, or diagonally as long as the cells touch each other.

6. Each player tries to form as many SOS lines as possible and to block the other player from doing so.

WINNER: The player with the most lines of SOS when the lattice is all filled up is the winner.

EXAMPLE: Here's an example of a mid-game situation where 5 SOS lines have been scored. Note that there is one SOS formed that neither player has seen yet. This is common. Either can now claim that SOS.

JOE (dashed): / / /
SAM (solid): / /

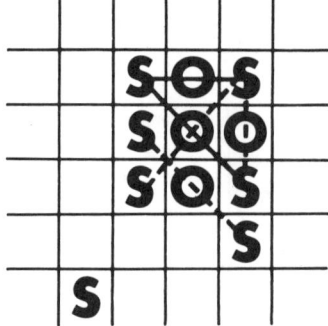

VARIATIONS:
1. Make the lattice 6 × 6 or even bigger for a long game.
2. Make the lattice 4 × 4 for a short game.

NOTE/COMMENT: If the players do not use different colors to draw their lines in order to keep them separate, then one can draw a double line or a dashed line. By the way, I learned this game from two youngsters from Teheran, Iran, who play it with their friends at home and in school. They both beat me in SOS, too.

DEBRIEFING HINTS: Focus on the strategy each player used to create a line of SOS; emphasize the need to plan ahead by thinking, "If I go here, he'll go there, and then I'll go there to make a line of SOS"; talk about the SOS lines formed but not noticed; discuss the phenomenon of missed opportunities before us that others might see but we ourselves don't see.

7

Paper, Pencil, Pennies— Like the Real World

AMBUSH

BENEFIT/PURPOSE: To enjoy a fast, tense simulation; to feel what it means to be watched; to predict and anticipate another person's moves; to feel what it means to have knowledge about another person without that person's knowing your moves.

MATERIALS: Paper and pencil to draw two identical gamesheets (see illustration); 2 pennies

NUMBER OF PARTICIPANTS: Two—one Scout and one Indian

Paper, Pencil, Pennies—Like the Real World

PROCEDURE:

1. Players decide who will be Scout and who will be Indian.

2. Players sit facing each other. Each player positions a gamesheet lengthwise, having the end with his/her role closer to him/her. Players place a barrier (several opaque large sheets of paper, for example) between the two gamesheets, set up in such a way that the Indian can still see the Scout's gamesheet as well as his/her own. The Scout can see only his/her own gamesheet and cannot see the Indian's gamesheet. In this way the Indian can see both gamesheets while the Scout can only see one, his/her own.

3. Each player puts a penny on his/her starting position: the Indian starts at Dot 23 and the Scout starts at Dot 2. The Scout's objective is to go safely from Dot 2 to his/her destination, which is Dot 22, or 23 or 24. The Indian's objective is to ambush the Scout anywhere along the way. The Indian ambushes the Scout

Paper, Pencil, Pennies—Like the Real World

when the Scout unknowingly lands on the numbered dot already occupied by the Indian. The Indian must thus anticipate where the Scout will move.

4. Players move alternately; the Indian moves first.

5. Each player moves his/her penny from dot to dot, one dot at a time in any direction along the lines of the gamesheet only.

6. Players must move on their turns.

7. The Scout and the Indian may move from any dot to any other dot connected by a line. However, the Indian, who can see the Scout's gamesheet, may not move onto the Scout's position (the same-numbered dot). That is to say, the Indian may not attack the Scout by moving onto a dot already occupied by the Scout. All other moves are permitted along the lines from dot to dot.

WINNER: If the Scout moves onto the Indian's position, even at Dot 22, 23, or 24, then the Indian announces that he/she has *ambushed the Scout* and shows the Scout his/her position. That is, the Indian wins when the Scout unknowingly moves onto the Indian's position as indicated by the same-numbered dot. If the Scout reaches Dot 22, or 23, or 24 safely, then the Scout wins. That is, the Scout has reached his/her destination and has not been ambushed by the Indian.

EXAMPLE: At the top of page 94 is an example of a game near the end. The Scout is on Dot 20, and the Indian is back on Dot 22. It's the Scout's move. If the Scout moves to Dot 23, then he/she wins. But if the Scout moves to Dot 22, then the Indian has ambushed the Scout and wins. Of course, the Scout can temporarily retreat to either Dot 15 or Dot 16 or move sideways to either Dot 19 or Dot 21.

VARIATIONS:

1. Every so often the players switch roles.

2. Change the labels of the roles for the players. Instead of Scout and Indian, use other labels appealing to your players. For example, Cop and Thief; FBI Agent and Drug Pusher; Principal and Student; Parent and Child; Counselor and Camper; Leader and Club Member.

AMBUSH!

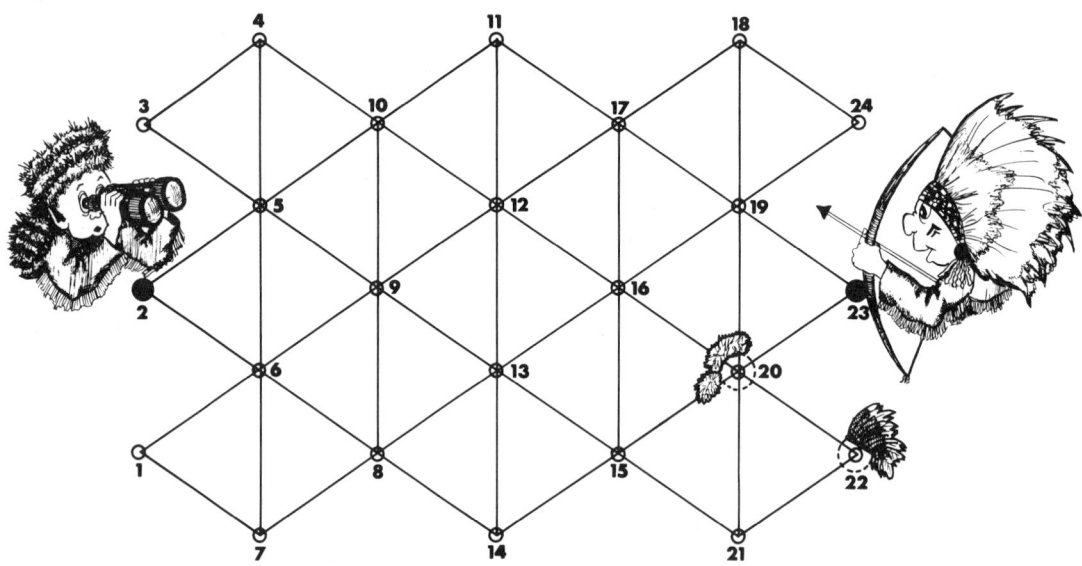

NOTE/COMMENT: In the way this game is set up, the Indian knows the Scout's movements and his/her own. The Indian, who may not attack, quietly waits for the Scout to fall into the Indian's ambush. The Indian must anticipate the Scout's moves just as the Scout must anticipate the Indian's moves. The Scout must cleverly predict the Indian's movements and then evade the Indian to reach his/her own destination safely at Dot 22, or 23, or 24, the end of the territory being scouted. The Scout knows that he/she is being watched by the Indian but still he/she must move on to his/her destination along the trails. Anticipation of the other person is the key.

DEBRIEFING HINTS: Talk about crucial moves and decisions; how it felt to know what another person was doing without that person knowing what you were doing; how it felt to be watched and waited for; what the best strategy is for the Scout; what the best strategy is for the Indian; who has the better opportunity to win, Scout or Indian; in what ways this game is parallel to the events in American history; what the lines and the space on the gamesheet represent in real life; what Dots 22, 23, and 24 represent; whether it makes sense to switch the labels of the two roles; what other pairs of roles fit this game.

LAND USE

BENEFIT/PURPOSE: To enjoy a game that projects us into the future; to learn that we have the opportunity to decide how we shall use the land available to us now and in the future; to learn that when we decide what to build on our land, we must also decide where to locate it; to understand empathically that various land uses affect different people in different ways.

MATERIALS: Pencil and paper; the two maps ("THIS YEAR" and "YEAR 2000") and role slips.

NUMBER OF PARTICIPANTS: At least 5, but preferably more

PROCEDURE:
   1. Distribute to each player a THIS YEAR map. (see page 96)
   2. Explain the map to the players; explain the layout; explain the choices available to them in terms of what 3 projects they can build and the 3 possible locations for each project.
   3. Give everyone a role slip describing a role (see the list of roles and their descriptions on pages 99 and 100). The 5 roles are ecologist, resident homeowner, builder, fisherman, and city mayor. Each has a specific objective and description as given on the role slips. If you form groups of 5 players before distributing the role slips, make sure you give one of each role to each group. If you distribute the roles first, then request players to group themselves so that there are 5 different roles in a group.

THIS YEAR

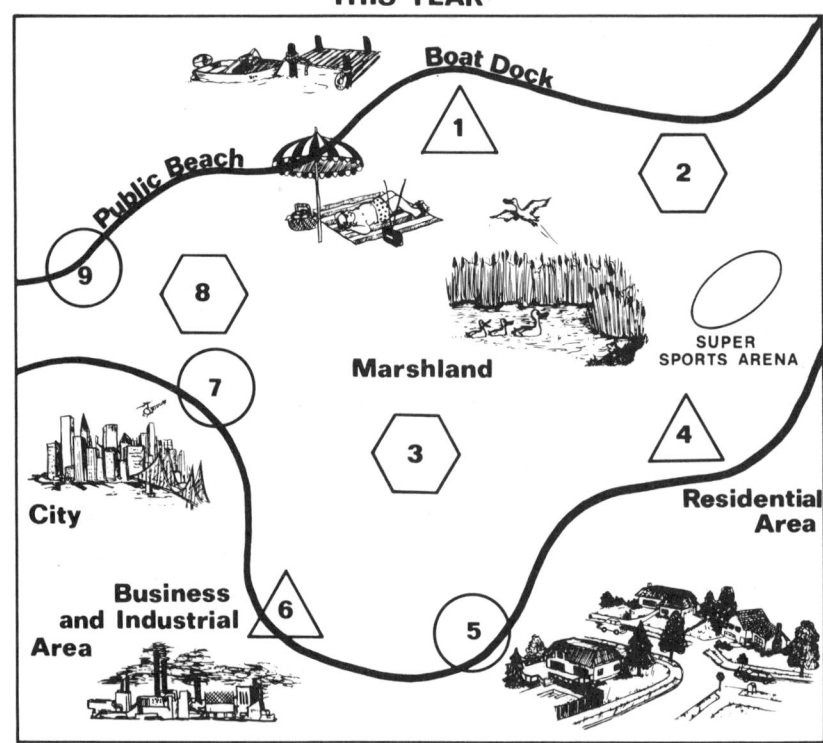

4. Ask players to study their role slips silently. Clarify any points to them. Here is the opportunity for players to learn what the 5 roles are by introducing themselves as ecologists, resident homeowners, builders, fishermen, and city mayors. Players should tell who they are, with only as much other information as they wish the rest of the players to know. They should not read their role slips aloud nor explicitly state their objectives to the group.

5. Have players individually and *silently* select two projects to build on the THIS YEAR map, given their specific roles. They may select any 2 of the possible 9 project locations by *coloring in the two symbols* on the map representing their two choices.

6. Ask players now to decide through discussion on two land uses and locations in their group. Each person is to participate according to his/her role. Give each city mayor an extra clean map on which to color in the group's decision. The two simple rules for

Paper, Pencil, Pennies—Like the Real World

this community-choice meeting are (a) everyone must strive to agree on the 2 project locations and (b) if the group cannot come to a unanimous decision, then the city mayor will decide for the group. The mayor will decide on the basis of the discussion points raised by the 5 players. Given the points raised by the group, the mayor is to decide on what is best for the community.

7. Post the results publicly on a chalkboard or easel pad. (See sample chart in the Example.)

8. Distribute to everyone a YEAR 2000 map.

9. Explain the map to the players; explain that the players are now in the future in the year 2000, that a steadily growing Super Sports Arena now exists near their community, that they had no control over the building of the Super Sport Arena because it was a state matter, and that now they have the opportunity to choose one more land-use project—a generating plant, an amusement park, a wildlife refuge, or a moon-rocket port.

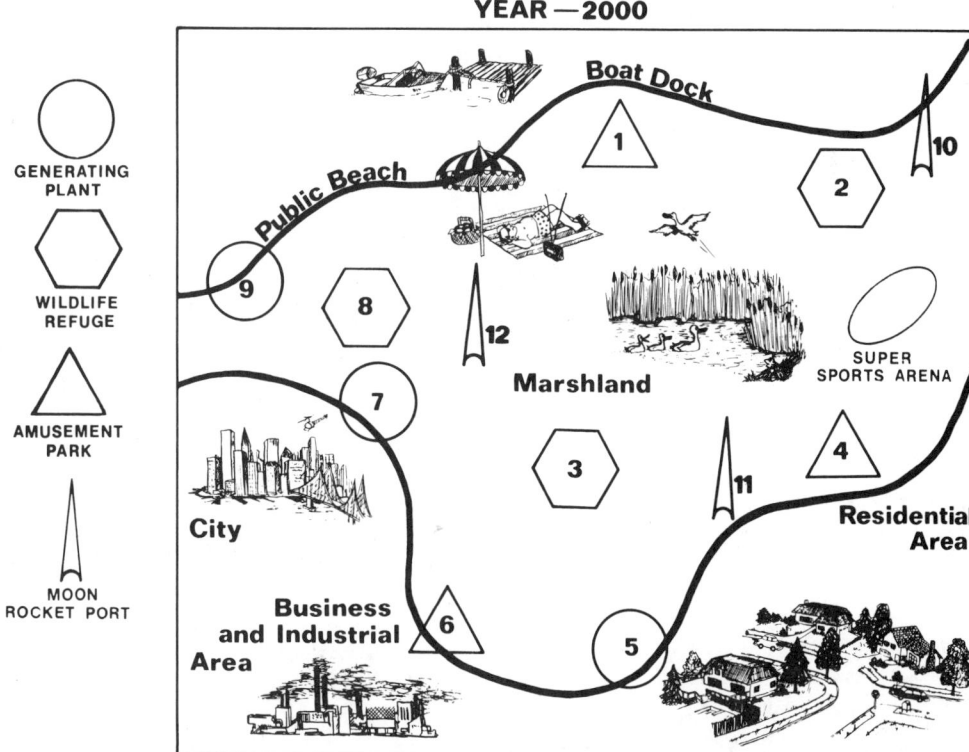

10. Players start by coloring in the two choices of their *group* from the THIS YEAR map. Then they may each color in individually and silently their own third choices, given their specific roles. They may choose any of the remaining 10 project locations.

11. Ask players in each community again to decide on a third choice by discussing it together. Give each city mayor an extra YEAR 2000 map on which to color in the groups decision. The group should strive for a unanimous decision. However, if one is not possible, this time a majority vote after 3 to 5 minutes will decide, (not the city mayor) as the laws of the city were changed recently (in 1998) to reduce the power of the mayor.

12. Post the YEAR 2000 results publicly and talk to the players about what happened. Debriefing is essential. See the Debriefing Hints.

WINNER: There is no winner in this simulation.

EXAMPLE: Here is the public record of a 3-group simulation showing the decisions made for the THIS YEAR and YEAR 2000 maps. The players were 10-year-old students.

	Group #1	*Group #2*	*Group #3*
THIS YEAR	Generating Plant 5 Amusement Park 6 100% agree.	Amusement Park 6 Wildlife Refuge 3 100% agree.	Generating Plant 7 Wildlife Refuge 8 City mayor decided.
YEAR 2000	Generating Plant 7 100% agree.	Moon Rocket Port 12 Majority vote.	Generating Plant 9 Majority vote.

VARIATIONS:

1. Allow 2 individual choices and 2 group choices for the YEAR 2000 map.

2. Rotate some players before distributing the YEAR 2000 map to create new groups.

3. Encourage the players to decorate an entire map.

NOTE/COMMENT: This simulation is deceptive in that it appears to be too simple to hold the players' attention. Yet, because it has many facets—land use; futurism, 3 different group decision-making processes, map reading, and map coloring—LAND USE can hold the attention of youngsters and even adults. The debriefing of this simulation shows how players decide and support their decisions. It is a sophisticated but easy simulation in which young people can demonstrate their concern for community planning now and in the future.

DEBRIEFING HINTS: After players look at the public record of all the groups' decisions, talk about how the various special interests influenced the group decisions; how the city mayor influenced or made the group's decision; what reasons the players use to support their decisions; why different groups have different decisions; how people feel about the roles they played; what problems your community faces in community planning; what possibilities will be available to us other than the moon-rocket port in the year 2000.

ROLE SLIPS

1. *Ecologist*—You are concerned with protecting nature. Your objective is to preserve the marshland.
2. *Resident homeowner*—You are the "average" resident. You live in a home on the edge of the marshland. Your objective is to do what you think is best for your city.
3. *Builder*—You have a family and have been out of work for six months. Your objective is to choose what will provide the most work for you.

4. *Fisherman*—You are a member of a fishing fleet. You and other fishermen support your families with the money you earn from fishing. You need the boat dock to tie up your boats and unload the day's catch. You were elected by the other fishermen to represent them to protect their fishing grounds and boat dock. Your objective is to preserve the boat dock and the fishing grounds.

5. *City mayor*—You are elected by the people to represent them. You are responsible for leading the people, especially in planning changes in the community. Your objective is to make your community a better place to live—a place for jobs and recreation for the people of the city.

WINTER CRASH SURVIVAL

BENEFIT/PURPOSE: To simulate the decisions of a survivor of a plane crash in winter; to learn about items necessary to a plane-crash survivor; to practice working with others in a small group; to compare two different methods of decision-making; to practice simple arithmetic skills of subtracting, adding, and dividing.

MATERIALS: Paper and pencil and Winter Crash Survival sheets for each participant. (This material follows the description of the game and must be reproduced.)

NUMBER OF PARTICIPANTS: 4 or more (If there are 8 or more participants, divide them into two or more small groups; from 4 to 7 is generally a good number for a small group. If there are more than 7 in a group, it is difficult to have maximum free communication.)

PROCEDURE:
1. Distribute the Individual Worksheets for the Winter Crash Survival; this worksheet gives the situation and the items saved.
2. Ask each person to read the sheet and correctly rank order the items independently. Encourage people to jot down notes as they rank the items. Allow 10 to 15 minutes for this activity.

Paper, Pencil, Pennies—Like the Real World

3. After all participants have finished ranking the 15 items, group the participants into small groups. Each group should consist of 4 to 7 people, as indicated before.

4. Distribute to each participant the Group Worksheet for the Winter Crash Survival. Review this worksheet with the participants, especially the Guidelines for Decision-Making by Consensus.

5. Request participants to follow the guidelines as they decide by group consensus. Each person should fill out a sheet listing the group's decisions to refer to later. (Obviously, each sheet this time will have the same rankings.) Allow 20 to 30 minutes for this activity.

6. When every group is finished with the Group Worksheet, distribute to every participant the Record Sheet for the Winter Crash Survival.

7. Ask everyone to copy into column 2 his/her rankings from the Individual Worksheet.

8. Ask everyone to compute his/her individual score in column 1. The score is the absolute difference between the person's ranking (column 2) and the correct ranking (column 3). Plus or minus signs do not count. For example, if for Item H (Knife) a person has a ranking of 6, then the score is 4 because the correct answer is 10. If the ranking for Item H is 14, the score is still 4. In either case, the person has placed Item H (Knife) 4 ranks away from the correct ranking, and the score is 4 for Item H (Knife).

9. When all participants are finished computing the Individual Score, ask them to follow a similar procedure for computing the Group Score on the right side of the Record Sheet in column 5 (the difference between columns 4 and 3.)

10. When the participants are finished computing the Group Score, ask them to compute the Average Individual Score and the Range by filling in the bottom part of the Record Sheet.

11. Post the results of each group's deliberation.

12. Talk with the participants about what happened. Debriefing is essential. See the Debriefing Hints for questions and information.

WINNER: There is no winner or loser in this simulation. The lower the score the better, however.

VARIATIONS:

1. Reduce the time allowed to better simulate an emergency situation.

2. Increase the time allowed to facilitate group interaction and group consensus.

NOTE/COMMENT: As with the Liver Transplant elsewhere in this book, this simulation involves two types of decision-making. Much of the benefit will come as participants discuss the 15 items and then later review what happened. Hence, the debriefing session is important to review the correct answers, the reasoning behind them, and the two types of decision-making processes.

DEBRIEFING HINTS: Talk about the Individual Scores, the Group Score, the Average Individual Score, and the Range of scores; which scores are better; what reasons there are for the differences; who gained by working in the group; who lost by working in the group; how many points were lost and how many gained by the group; what the data mean regarding the two types of decision-making.

Talk about the reasoning behind the correct rankings of the 15 items. For this discussion see the Background Information and Scoring Key.

BACKGROUND INFORMATION FOR WINTER CRASH SURVIVAL

Note: None of the information here should be given to participants until after they have completed the decision-making parts of the exercise.

Mid-January is the coldest time of the year in Minnesota and Manitoba. The first problem the survivors face, therefore, is to preserve their body heat and protect themselves against its loss. This problem can be met by building a fire, minimizing movement and exertion, and using as much insulation as possible.

The participants have just crash-landed. Many individuals tend to overlook the enormous shock reaction that has upon the human body, and the death of the pilot and copilot increases the shock. Decision-making under such conditions is extremely difficult. Such a situation requires a strong emphasis upon the use of reasoning, not only to make decisions, but also to reduce the fear and panic every person would naturally feel. Along with fear, shock reaction is manifested in feelings of helplessness, loneliness, and hopelessness. These feelings have brought about more fatalities than perhaps any other cause in survival situations. Through the use of reasoning, hope for survival and the will to live can be generated. Certainly the state of shock means that movement of individuals should be at a minimum and that an attempt to calm them should be made.

Before taking off a pilot always has to file a flight plan. The flight plan contains the vital information regarding the flight, such as the course, speed, estimated time of arrival, type of aircraft, number of people on board, and so on. Search-and-rescue operations would begin shortly after the plane failed to arrive at its destination at its estimated time of arrival.

The eighty miles to the nearest known town is a very long walk even under ideal conditions, particularly if one is not used to walking such distances. Under the circumstances of being in shock, dressed in city clothes, having deep snow in the woods and a variety of water barriers to cross, to attempt to walk out would mean almost certain death from freezing and exhaustion. At the temperatures given, the loss of body heat through exertion is a very serious matter.

Once the survivors have found ways in which to keep warm, their most immediate problem is to provide signaling methods to attract the attention of search planes and search parties. Thus, all the items the group has must be assessed according to their value in signaling the group's whereabouts.

SCORING KEY

The correct ranking of the survivors' items was made on the basis of information provided by Mark Wanig and supplemented from *The New Way of the Wilderness,* by C. Rutstrum (New York: Collier, 1973). Wanig was an instructor for three years in survival training in the reconnaissance school in the 101st Division of the U. S. Army and later an instructor on wilderness survival for four years at the Twin City Institute for Talented Youth. He is now conducting wilderness-survival programs for Minneapolis teachers.

Rank 1. *Cigarette lighter (without fluid).* The gravest danger facing the group is exposure to the cold. The greatest need is for a source of warmth, and the second greatest need is for signaling devices. This makes building a fire the first order of business.

Without matches something is needed to produce sparks to start a fire. Even without fluid the cigarette lighter can be used to produce sparks. The fire will not only provide warmth, it will also provide smoke for daytime signaling and firelight for nighttime signaling.

Rank 2. *Ball of steel wool.* To make a fire, a means of catching the sparks made by the cigarette lighter is needed. Steel wool is the best substance with which to catch a spark and support a flame, even if it is a little bit wet.

Rank 3. *Extra shirt and pants for each survivor.* Clothes are probably the most versatile items one can have in a situation like this. Besides adding warmth to the body they can be used for shelter, signaling, bedding, bandages, string when unraveled, and tinder to make fires. Maps can even be drawn on them. The versatility of clothes and the need for fires, signaling devices, and warmth make this item number three in importance.

Rank 4. *Family-size chocolate bar (one per person).* To gather wood for the fire and to set up signals, energy is needed. The chocolate bars would supply the energy to sustain the survivors for quite some time. Because they contain basically carbohydrates, they would supply energy without making digestive demands upon the body.

Rank 5. *Can of shortening.* This item has many uses—the most important being that a mirrorlike signaling device can be made from the lid. After shining the lid with the steel wool, the survivors can use it to produce an effective reflector of sunlight. A mirror is the most powerful tool they have for communicating their presence. In sunlight, a simple mirror can generate 5 to 7 million candlepower. The reflected sunbeam can be seen beyond the horizon. Its effectiveness is somewhat limited by the trees, but one member of the group could climb a tree and use the mirror to signal search planes. If the survivors have no other means of signaling, they would still have a better than 80 percent chance of being rescued within the first twenty-four hours.

Other uses for the item are as follows: Shortening can be rubbed on the body to protect exposed areas, such as the face, lips, and hands, from the cold. In desperation it could be eaten in small amounts. When melted into oil, shortening is helpful in starting fires. Melted shortening, when soaked into a piece of cloth, will produce an effective candlewick. The can is useful in melting snow to produce drinking water. Even in the winter, water is important as the body loses water in many ways such as perspiration, respiration, shock reactions, and so on. This water must be replenished because dehydration affects the ability to make clear decisions. The can is also useful as a cup.

Rank 6. *Flashlight with batteries.* Inasmuch as the group has little hope of survival if it decides to walk out, its major hope is to catch the attention of search planes. During the day the lid-mirror, smoke, and flags made from clothing represent the best devices. During the night the flashlight is the best signaling device. It is the only effective night-signaling device besides the fire. In the cold, however, a flashlight loses the power in its battery very quickly. It must therefore, be kept warm if it is to work, which means that it must be kept close to someone's body. The value of the flashlight lies in the fact that if the fire burns low or inadvertently is allowed to go out, the flashlight could be immediately turned on the moment a plane is heard.

Rank 7. *30 feet of rope.* The rope is another versatile piece of equipment. It could be used to pull dead limbs off trees for firewood. When cut into pieces, the rope will help in constructing shelters. It can be burned. When frayed it can be used as tinder to start fires. When unraveled it will make good insulation from the cold if it is stuffed inside clothing.

Rank 8. *Newspaper (one per person).* The newspaper could be used for starting a fire in much the same way as the rope. It will also serve as an insulator; when rolled up and placed under the clothes around a person's legs or arms, it provides dead-air space for extra protection from the cold. The paper can be used for recreation by reading it, memorizing it, folding it, or tearing it. It could be rolled into a cone and yelled through as a signal device. It could also be spread around an area to help signal a rescue party.

Rank 9. *Loaded .45-caliber pistol.* This pistol provides a sound-signaling device. (The international distress signal is three shots fired in rapid succession.) There have been numerous cases of survivors going undetected because by the time the rescue party arrived in the area the survivors were too weak to make a loud enough noise to attract attention. The butt of the pistol could be used as a hammer. The powder from the shells will assist in fire building. By placing a small bit of cloth in a cartridge, emptied of its bullet, a fire can be started by firing the gun at dry wood on the ground. At night the muzzle blast of the gun is visible, which also makes it useful as a signaling device.

The pistol's advantages are counterbalanced by its dangerous disadvantages. Anger, frustration, impatience, irritability, and lapses of rationality may increase as the group waits to be rescued. The availability of a lethal weapon is a real danger to the group under these conditions. Although a gun could be used for hunting, it would take a highly skilled marksman to kill an animal, and then the animal would have to be transported through the snow to the crash area, probably taking more energy than would be advisable.

Rank 10. *Knife.* A knife is a versatile tool, but it is not too important in the winter setting. It could be used for cutting the rope into desired lengths and making shavings from pieces of wood for tinder; many other uses could be thought up.

Rank 11. *Compress kit (with gauze).* The best use of this item is to wrap the gauze around exposed areas of the body for insulation. Feet and hands are probably the most vulnerable to frostbite, and the gauze can be used to keep them warm. The gauze can be used as a candle wick when dipped into melted shortening. It would also make effective tinder. The small supply of the gauze is the reason this item is ranked so low.

Rank 12. *Two ski poles.* Although they are not very important, the poles are useful as a flagpole or staff for signaling. They can be used to stabilize a person walking through the snow to collect wood, and to test the thickness of the ice on a lakeshore or stream.

Probably their most useful function would be as supports for a shelter or by the fire for a heat reflector.

Rank 13. *Quart of 85-proof whiskey.* The only useful function of the whiskey is to aid in fire building or as a fuel. A torch could be made from a piece of clothing soaked in the whiskey and attached to an upright ski pole. The danger of the whiskey is that someone might try to drink it when it is cold. Whiskey takes on the temperature it is exposed to, and a drink of it at minus thirty degrees would freeze a person's esophagus and stomach and do considerable damage to the mouth. Drinking it warm will cause dehydration. The empty bottle, kept warm, would be useful for storing drinking water.

Rank 14. *Sectional air map made of plastic.* This item is dangerous because it will encourage individuals to attempt to walk to the nearest town, thereby condemning them to almost certain death.

Rank 15. *Compass.* Because the compass may also encourage some survivors to try to walk to the nearest town, it too is a dangerous item. The only redeeming feature of the compass is the possible use of its glass top as a reflector of sunlight to signal search planes, but it is the least effective of the potential signaling devices available. That it might tempt survivors to walk away from the crash site makes it the least desirable of the fifteen items.

WINTER CRASH SURVIVAL

INDIVIDUAL WORKSHEET

You have just crash-landed in the woods of North Minnesota and Southern Manitoba. It is 11:32 a.m. in mid-January. The small plane in which you were traveling has been completely destroyed except for the frame. The pilot and the copilot have been killed, but no one else is seriously injured.

Paper, Pencil, Pennies—Like the Real World

The crash came suddenly before the pilot had time to radio for help or inform anyone of your position. Because your pilot was trying to avoid a storm, you know the plane was considerably off course. The pilot announced shortly before the crash that you were eighty miles northwest of a small town that is the nearest known habitation.

You are in a wilderness area made up of thick woods broken by many lakes and rivers. The last weather report indicated that the temperature would reach minus 25 degrees in the daytime and minus 40 at night. You are dressed in winter clothing appropriate for city wear—suits, pantsuits, street shoes, and overcoats.

You may assume that the number of survivors is the same as the number of people in your group and that the group has agreed to stick together.

While escaping from the plane your group salvaged the fifteen items listed here. Your task is to rank these items according to their importance to your group's survival, starting with "1" for the most important and proceeding to "15" for the least important:

- A._____Compress kit (with 28 feet of 2-inch gauze)
- B._____Ball of steel wool
- C._____Cigarette lighter (without fluid)
- D._____Loaded .45-caliber pistol
- E._____Newspaper (one per person)
- F._____Compass
- G._____Two ski poles
- H._____Knife
- I._____Sectional air map made of plastic
- J._____30 feet of rope
- K._____Family-size chocolate bar (one per person)
- L._____Flashlight with batteries
- M._____Quart of 85-proof whiskey
- N._____Extra shirt and pants for each survivor
- O._____Can of shortening

WINTER CRASH SURVIVAL

Paper, Pencil, Pennies—Like the Real World

GROUP WORKSHEET

This is an exercise in group decision-making for the Winter Crash Survival situation. Your group is to employ the method of group consensus to reach its decision. This means that the ranking for each of the 15 survival items must be agreed upon by each group member before it becomes a part of the group decision. Consensus is difficult to reach. Therefore, not every ranking will meet with everyone's complete approval. Nevertheless, try as a group to make each ranking one with which all group members can at least partially agree. Here are four Guidelines for Decision-Making by consensus:

1. Avoid arguing for your own individual judgments. Approach the task on the basis of reason.
2. Avoid changing your mind only to reach agreement and to avoid conflict. Support only decisions with which you are able to agree somewhat.
3. Avoid conflict-reducing techniques such as majority vote, averaging, or trading your decisions.
4. View differences of opinion as helpful to, rather than as hindering, good decision-making.

Here are the 15 items:

A._____Compress kit (with 28 feet of 2-inch gauze)
B._____Ball of steel wool
C._____Cigarette lighter (without fluid)
D._____Loaded .45-caliber pistol
E._____Newspaper (one per person)
F._____Compass
G._____Two ski poles
H._____Knife
I._____Sectional air map made of plastic
J._____30 feet of rope

K._____Family-size chocolate bar (one per person)
L._____Flashlight with batteries
M._____Quart of 85-proof whiskey
N._____Extra shirt and pants for each survivor
O._____Can of shortening

WINTER CRASH SURVIVAL RECORD SHEET

Item	My Individual Score	My Ranking	Correct Ranking	My Ranking	My Group's Score
A			11		
B			2		
C			1		
D			9		
E			8		
F			15		
G			12		
H			10		
I			14		
J			7		
K			4		
L			6		
M			13		
N			3		
O			5		
TOTAL		← My Individual Score		My Group Score →	

} Individual Scores of others in my group

{ Grand total of all Individual Scores, including my own, in my group
{ Average Individual Score (Grand Total ÷ number of people in my group, including myself)

Range of Individual Scores in my group is from a low score of ☐
to a high score of ☐

CAR RACING

Paper, Pencil, Pennies—Like the Real World

BENEFIT/PURPOSE: To enjoy a unique, exciting, and competitive racing game; to understand the concepts of acceleration and deceleration in car racing (and ordinary driving as well); to understand the concept of momentum, especially as it applies to taking curves; to appreciate the skill and danger involved in car racing; to improve perception of space by relating speed and distance.

MATERIALS: Paper and pencil; paper with graph lines (see Example) and preferably a pencil of a different color for each player.

NUMBER OF PARTICIPANTS: 2 or 3 per race track; in a large group there can be many races going on at separate tables simultaneously. (SEE NOTE/COMMENT section.)

PROCEDURE:

1. Have pairs or trios of players draw their own unbanked tracks, which they will race on. (Show some of your own tracks as examples. Keep the track wide and simple, especially at first. Here are some sample tracks in miniature. See also the horseshoe-shaped track in the Example section.)

2. Ask players to decide on their starting positions on the track.

Start   Finish   Start   Finish   Start   Finish   Start   Finish

3. Explain to the players that they race according to these 5 simple rules (see Example for clarification):

   a. Players move alternately if there are 2 racers and in rotation if there are 3 or 4 racers.
   b. Each line represents 10 mph; you move from one point (the vertex of 2 lines) to another as you choose. You can on each turn increase your speed 10 mph, decrease it 10 mph, or maintain the same speed as on your previous turn in one direction or two directions, independently.
   c. You can go in one direction only (north or south or west or east only), or you can go in two directions (north and east, north and west, south and east, south and west) at the same time. There is no single diagonal direction. You go on a diagonal in order to take a curve by going in two directions.
   d. No two racers may be on the same point at the same time. That is, you may not cause a collision with another car by landing on the same point as a car ahead of you occupies. You may cross another car's path, however. If you *must* collide with another car on your next turn, then you are out of the race.
   e. Your new position and the straight line connecting this point with your former position must be entirely within the course. That is, if you cannot take a curve successfully and leave the track at any time, you are out of the race. Thus, "crashing the wall" means you have died in the race.

Now, it follows from these rules that speed and direction are linked together just as in bike racing and horse racing. At every move, at whatever point you are, you must decide on both speed and direction. If you decide to accelerate or decelerate in the direction you're going, you can do so only by 10 mph in a single turn. Thus (on the race track in the Example section) the first move is 10 mph N, or 10 mph N and 10 mph E, or 10 mph N and 10 mph W. Now, if you are going 30 mph north, for example, then on your next turn you must go 40 mph N (accelerate 10), 30 mph N (stay the same), or 20 mph N (decelerate 10). That is all you can do about going north. You cannot speed up to 50 mph or more north or slow down to 10 mph or less north on that single turn.

Paper, Pencil, Pennies—Like the Real World

If you are going in only one direction you can start going in two directions on your next move. (This is how you take a curve.) But you can only start with 10 mph in that new direction. See Dashed's moves 10 through 18 in the example. (Move 10 is the line between points 9 and 10; move 18 is the line between points 17 and 18.) The two directions work independently. For example, if on your last turn you went 30 mph north only, on your next turn in addition to 20 or 30 or 40 mph N you can go 10 mph east or 10 mph west. Of course, you can decide to continue going North only.

If you went two directions on your last turn, then on your next turn you can accelerate, decelerate, or maintain your speed in each of the two directions. For example, if you went 30 mph N and 20 mph E (as Dashed does on move 11 in the Example), then on your next turn you must go:

20 mph N and 10, 20, or 30 mph E,
or 30 mph N and 10, 20, or 30 mph E,
or 40 mph N and 10, 20, or 30 mph E.

Dashed on the next move, move 12, chooses to go 20 mph N and 20 mph E. The two directions are independent (and the sums of the two directions don't need to balance each other arithmetically with a previous move).

You obviously cannot reverse directions without slowing down to zero mph first, just as in bike racing. That is, you cannot switch from north to south, for example, without slowing down to 0 mph N first. Once you slow down to 0 mph N, then you can begin speeding up 10 mph south at every turn if you wish. See Dashed's moves 13 through 15 in the Example.

These rules prohibit a very sharp turn in any direction at high speeds as well as an immediate reversal of directions. This is to simulate real-life racing on a flat track, where a quick turn or reversal results in a spill. Great momentum in any direction in a

Paper, Pencil, Pennies—Like the Real World

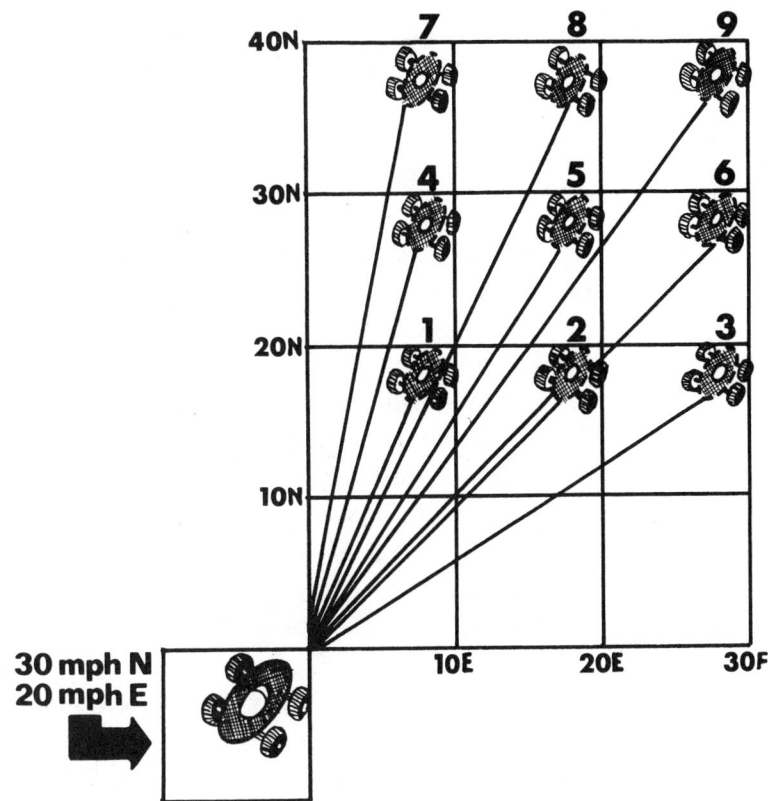

9 Choices

car carries you forward as you slow down, forcing you to take a wide, bad turn around a curve. This is what happens to solid in the Example. A poor turn on the curve, moves 9 through 15, causes solid to lose the race. For example, if you are going only north, or both north and east, you cannot head east only until you slow down to 0 mph N. If you're going too fast north, then you won't be able to take the curve to the right. You'll crash the wall and be out of the race.

WINNER: The first racer to touch or to cross the finish line is the winner (or the racer farthest from the finish line if two racers cross the line in the same round).

EXAMPLE: Here is a complete 2-car race won by the Dashed racer. Neither driver took the curve at the northwest corner of the track well. Dashed wins on move 22, 2 moves ahead of solid, by just touching the finish line going 80 mph south.

VARIATIONS:
1. Draw a shorter and simpler track for an easier race; a longer and more complex track for a harder race.
2. For a harder and more realistic race, draw an oil patch on the track; cars must maintain their speed and direction when passing through it.
3. Draw the starting line on a slant to compensate for the outside starting position (as in real-life racing.)

NOTE/COMMENT: This is a complex game at the outset. It gets very easy after 1 or 2 short races, however. Young players, as young as 10 years old, can effectively play Car Racing. At first, however, they need much supervision as they learn how to take curves that are especially difficult for them to maneuver. Therefore, it is advisable for you to play with young players at first to help them master the rules.

DEBRIEFING HINTS: Talk about the various moves (and strategies) each racer made; the concept of momentum of a moving object, especially a fast and heavy vehicle; that it is impossible to brake a car and bring it to an immediate stop when it is going 50 mph, for example; that a car can accelerate but does so slowly rather than immediately (that is, you can't go from a parked position to 50 mph immediately); that there are dangers connected with high speed; that sharp turns are impossible at high speeds.

Race Track

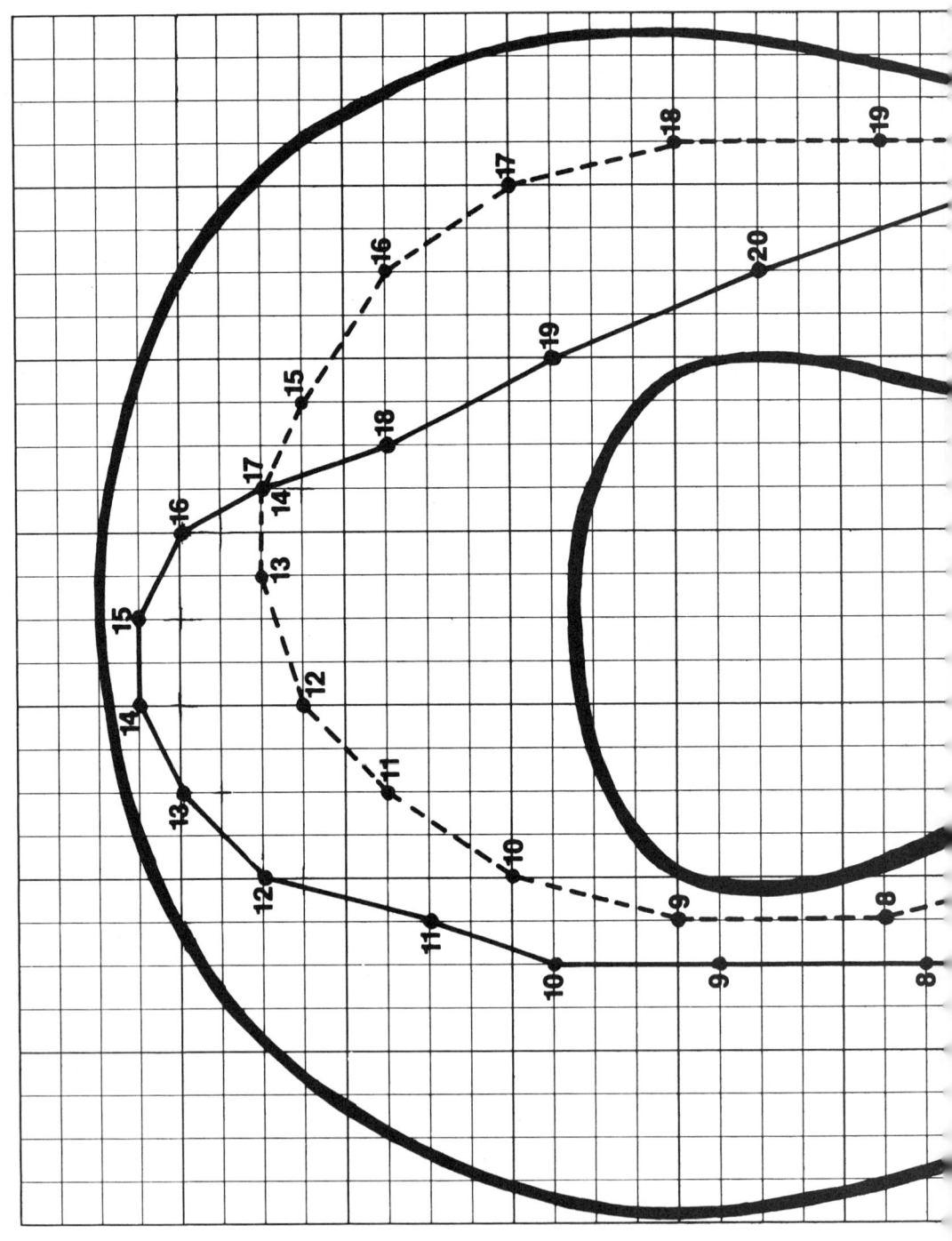

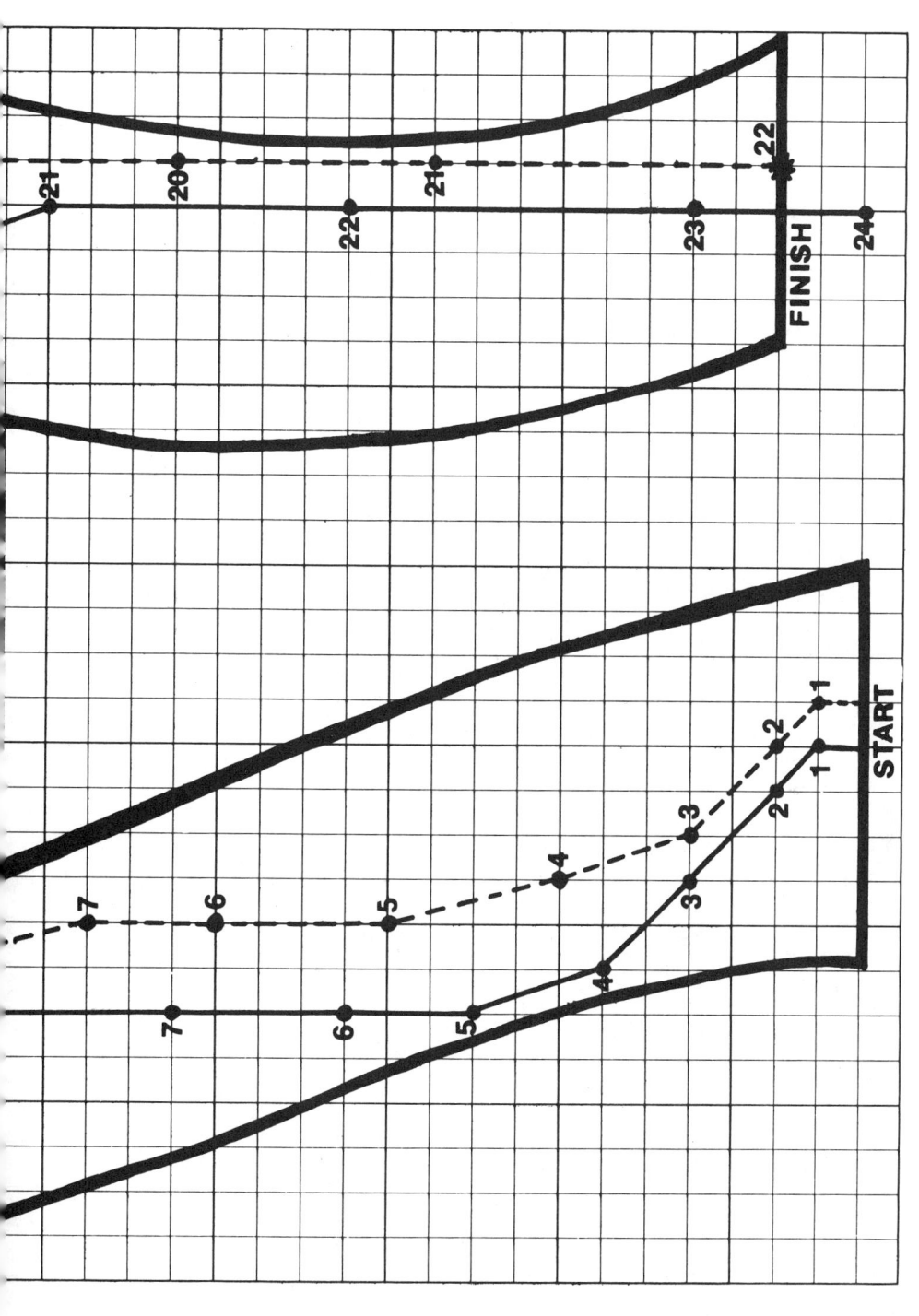

HUNGRY ZENOBIANS

Paper, Pencil, Pennies—Like the Real World

BENEFIT/PURPOSE: To simulate the effects of the maldistribution of food in the world even when an overall limited but adequate food supply exists; to realize the relationship between death, starvation, and affluece; to understand the consequences of cooperation and competition, as well as caring and indifference, in regard to food consumption; to develop empathy for those people without sufficient food; to internalize the ramifications of a food shortage.

MATERIALS: Paper, pencil, and pennies. Paper and pencil if a chalkboard is not available for posting a Public Chart, and a Gold Star Chart for creating wearable DEAD signs or badges (about 1 for every two participants) and wearable GOLD STAR signs or badges (about 1 for every two participants). Pennies to serve as gramma (4 per participant; these all might be shiny, or all of one particular date, or all colored with a marker on one side, or all in some other way easily identifiable as "gramma" if participants have their own pennies available).

NUMBER OF PARTICIPANTS: 7 to 30

PROCEDURE:

1. Prepare the room by arranging the furniture randomly to allow participants to move about freely. Prepare a blank Public Chart on a chalkboard or large sheet of paper. Make the chart big enough to record every participant's name. (See Step 6 for the headings of the Public Chart.) Prepare a Gold Star Chart to aid you in describing how a participant may receive a GOLD STAR. (See Step 4D for the heading for the Gold Star Chart.)

2. Spread the gramma around the room in clusters of differing amounts.

3. Read aloud the Scenario for the Hungry Zenobians. Read slowly so that participants will understand the scenario as they listen. Simplify and elucidate when necessary.

4. Review the following rules from the scenario:

   a. You may not speak or sit, that is, you must stand and remain silent.
   b. You must consume at least one gramma every four minutes in order to live. The consumption of gramma is shown by giving one gramma to the leader, who will keep records on the gramma.
   c. If you starve and die, you will wear a DEAD sign as you stand around the edge of the room.
   d. You may obtain a GOLD STAR if you have extra gramma according to the GOLD STAR Chart. If you have a GOLD STAR, you may sit down and talk to other Zenobians with a GOLD STAR only.

FOR A GOLD STAR	
After turning in gramma at end of	You need on hand at least
Round 1	5 gramma
Round 2	4 gramma
Round 3	3 gramma
Round 4	2 gramma

5. After the rules are clear, announce simply, "You may all stand and silently begin your search for gramma." (Do not attempt to regulate the participants' behavior. See Note/Comment section.

6. After four minutes announce that it is time to consume gramma, shown by turning in one gramma. Call off each participant's name individually, asking for one gramma and the number of gramma still on hand. Record the information in a Public Chart for all to see, either on a chalkboard or a big poster sheet. The chart should resemble the table at the top of page 123. Record in the column marked Round 1 whether or not a participant has turned in one gramma or has died.

NAME	GRAMMA ROUND 1 ON HAND	GRAMMA ROUND 2 ON HAND	GRAMMA ROUND 3 ON HAND	GRAMMA ROUND 4 ON HAND
1.				
2.				
3.				

7. If a participant has died, give him/her a DEAD sign to wear. That person is to stand at the edge of the room. If a participant has 5 gramma on hand, give him/her a GOLD STAR to wear.

8. Proceed in the same manner for 3 more rounds. Collect gramma, give out DEAD signs, give out GOLD STARS, and collect GOLD STARS whenever appropriate, according to the Public Chart and the GOLD STAR requirements chart. Decrease or increase the time allocated for each round as you see fit, in order to make this simulation flow smoothly. If anyone exercises the privileges of the GOLD STAR without the right to do so, report it to the rightful GOLD STAR Zenobians, admonish him/her, or play it by ear.

9. At the conclusion of Round 4, when gramma are turned in and the data recorded in the Public Chart, declare that the living Zenobians will continue to live since scientists have succeeded in their research efforts.

10. Talk with the participants about what happened. Debriefing is essential. See the Debriefing Hints section.

WINNER: There is no winner or loser in this simulation.

VARIATIONS:

1. Shorten or lengthen the time for each round of play.

2. Increase or decrease the amount of available gramma, depending on whether you wish to create an abundance or a shortage in the supply of food for the planet.

3. Extend the play for a Round 5, claiming that the Zenobian scientists did not succeed in creating gramma in their laboratories. Base your decision on the data in the Public Chart column marked "gramma on hand" at the end of Round 4. Be cautious here, as most participants might die after Round 5.

NOTE/COMMENT: In large measure the success of this simulation depends upon the spontaneity of the reactions of the participants. For this reason you should give the Zenobians as few hints as possible concerning the nature of the HUNGRY ZENOBIANS in

advance of play. Participants will need to communicate nonverbally that they want to receive or give gramma to each other. After Round 1, participants with zero gramma on hand must obtain a gramma from someone, or they will die at the end of Round 2. Keep an eye on these Zenobians. This is a powerful simulation.

DEBRIEFING HINTS: Talk about who survived and who died by starvation; how the participants obtained their gramma (collected, begged, received a gift, stole, robbed); how they felt about impending death by starvation and watching others die by starvation; how the dead felt when they died knowing that others could have saved them; how the GOLD STAR Zenobians felt when others died when they themselves had extra gramma; who helped others to live; who organized the Zenobians to create a just distribution of gramma so that all could live (if there are 4 gramma per participant, there is no built-in reason for anyone to die at the end of Round 4); how the activity of the Zenobians is similar to that of humans on Earth regarding the distribution and consumption of food.

SOURCE: This simulation was created by Toyce Collins and Carolyn Pagel in my simulations class at Rutgers University.

SCENARIO FOR THE HUNGRY ZENOBIANS

For a short time you are all living on the planet Zenobia and are members of the Zenobian race. As Zenobians you are human-like beings. As you begin your life on Zenobia you are unable to speak and unable to sit.

Much of your life on Zenobia will be devoted to searching for, storing, and consuming a special substance called gramma. The consumption of one gramma every four minutes provides you with all of your nourishment to live. In times of plenty, collection and consumption of gramma are easy and carefree. However, lately it has become a bit difficult to collect gramma. Days of plenty are over, and some Zenobians are miserable because they may not get enough gramma to live long. When a Zenobian does not consume gramma on time, the result is a quick death.

Despite these conditions, the future holds a ray of hope. Zenobian scientists feel confident that in a very short time they will be able to create much gramma in their laboratories. However, until the scientists succeed, Zenobians must continue to consume one gramma every 4 minutes. Thus, if Zenobians can each consume 4 gramma during the next 16 minutes or so from their own stockpiles, or from continued searching, or from other Zenobians, they will continue to live a long, gramma-filled life. Whoever does not consume a gramma on time will die immediately.

One additional feature of Zenobian life deserves mention. All Zenobians must stand and remain silent as they search for gramma except for those Zenobians who have a GOLD STAR. Zenobians with a GOLD STAR may sit down when they please and may talk, but only to other GOLD STAR Zenobians, during the next round. Anyone can get a GOLD STAR if he/she has a stockpile of gramma according to the GOLD STAR chart. (Show the Gold Star Chart.) Since you are new to the planet Zenobia, you may get a GOLD STAR only after you consume your first gramma in four minutes. After that, you may gain or lose your GOLD STAR depending on your stockpile on hand.

Anyone who exercises the privileges of a Gold Star Zenobian but does not have a GOLD STAR will be dealt with in an appropriate manner. There are gramma spread around the planet Zenobia.

Liver Transplant

BENEFIT/PURPOSE: To simulate a hospital policy committee that has the power of life and death over people; to raise moral questions concerning a person's worth; to learn and practice skill in deciding by consensus; to practice working with others in a small group.

127

Paper, Pencil, Pennies—Like the Real World

MATERIALS: Paper and pencil and a LIVER TRANSPLANT scenario for each participant (see text that follows for scenario and explanation of the importance of the liver).

NUMBER OF PARTICIPANTS: 4 or more. (If there are 8 or more participants, divide them into two or more small groups; from 4 to 7 is generally a good number for a small group. If there are more than 7 in a group, it is difficult to have maximum free communication.)

PROCEDURE:
1. Distribute the LIVER TRANSPLANT scenario giving the Instructions and listing the Seven Applicants.
2. Ask each person to read the sheet and decide individually which 3 people he/she chooses to receive the liver transplant. Each person should circle the numbers of the 3 chosen applicants. Encourage people to jot down notes as they decide on the applicants. Allow 5 to 10 minutes.
3. After all participants have finished indicating their decisions, group the participants into committees. Each committee should consist of 4 to 7 people.
4. Ask each committee to decide now together by *consensus* which 3 people will receive liver transplants. Allow 20 to 35 minutes. To aid the committee, list on the board or give out a sheet with the following four Guidelines for Decision-Making by Consensus:

   a. Avoid arguing for your own individual judgments. Approach the task on the basis of reason.
   b. Avoid changing your mind only to reach agreement and to avoid conflict. Support only decisions with which you are able to agree somewhat.
   c. Avoid conflict-reducing techniques such as majority vote, averaging, or trading in reaching your decision.
   d. View differences of opinion as helpful to, rather than as hindering, good decision-making.

5. Post the results of each committee's deliberation.

6. Talk with the participants about what happened. Debriefing is essential. See the Debriefing Hints section for questions and information.

WINNER: There is no winner or loser in this simulation.

VARIATIONS:
 1. Change the descriptions of the 7 applicants to suit your participants, either entirely or in part.
 2. Have the participants select 4 or 2 applicants only.

3. After the participants have selected their applicants, ask them to rank order the ones not chosen to form Alternates—#1 being first alternate, #2 second alternate, and so forth—in case of premature death among the chosen applicants.

NOTE/COMMENT: Much of the benefit from this simulation will come as the participants talk over the issues in committee and then all together talk about their decision-making later, as in the Winter Crash Survival activity elsewhere in this book. There will be much discussion in each committee because the chances of complete initial agreement by the committee people are slim. Hence, the debriefing session on the Liver Transplant is especially important.

DEBRIEFING HINTS AND EXPLANATION: Talk about which applicants were saved by the participants individually and in committee; which applicants were "put to death"; how it felt to have the power of life or death over another person; what makes a person worthwhile to save; what criteria you used in saving a person's life; whether it was difficult to reach a consensus decision; how you handled differences of opinion in your committee; whom the committee represents in real life; what advice we would offer our community health people; what exactly a liver transplant does that it can help save a person's life.

The liver is the largest organ of the body beside the skin. It is absolutely necessary for life. When the liver stops functioning, death occurs within a matter of days. The liver frees the blood, as it passes through the liver, of its waste matter and poisons. It produces bile, which is used in digesting food. The liver also makes and stores the chemicals that are needed to turn food into energy for our bodies. It produces proteins that are necessary to build our muscles and to keep our blood healthy. Thus, the liver, though not as well understood by most people as is the heart, is a complex and vital organ.

Just as it became possible in past years to transplant hearts and kidneys, so we may now be on the verge of a medical breakthrough with the liver. We are seeing the development of liver transplants today, just as we looked forward to heart transplants in the early 1960s and to kidney transplants in the years before that.

SOURCE: Thanks to Professor David B. Sachar, M.D., of the Mount Sinai Medical School in New York City for consulting with me in the design of this Liver Transplant simulation.

SCENARIO FOR THE LIVER TRANSPLANT SIMULATION

INSTRUCTIONS: You have been chosen to serve on a hospital committee to decide which of seven applicants are to receive a liver transplant. The operation for transplanting a pig liver into a human has been improved to the point that it is now possible for the first time to save the lives of people who would otherwise die of liver diseases. Your hospital is the only one in the world where this operation can be successfully performed. Because the procedure is so costly and complex, however, only three transplants can be performed each year. You must choose, therefore, only three of the seven applicants.

Keep in mind three important considerations:

1. The applicants are all suffering from a rapidly growing liver tumor. Without a liver transplant all will die within a year.
2. No one can share a liver with anyone else.
3. You are the final authority in this case—you cannot delegate the decision to anyone else.

SEVEN APPLICANTS:
1. White 29-year-old female bank robber with 6 children, the oldest of whom is 12 years old; on welfare ever since she was released from prison last year.

2. White 70-year-old Swiss businessman (manufactures watches). Family will donate $3,200,000 to research on liver diseases if he is chosen to get a transplant.
3. Seventeen year-old delinquent with a high IQ but a 3-year drug (nonaddictive) history; currently unemployed.
4. White female physician 54 years old—works half time in community health clinic; her other work involves research on vaccines for infectious diseases; had mild heart attack 2 years ago.
5. Black female college scholarship student, age 21, who is carrier of sickle-cell anemia.
6. Male musician, age 36, famous concert violinist and teacher.
7. Oriental male orphan, 4 years old; otherwise healthy and seemingly bright.

Expressway

BENEFIT/PURPOSE: To illustrate and feel the impact of various social-interest groups on governmental officials responsible for planning expressway routes; to engage in and develop negotiation skills (resolution of conflict skills).

MATERIALS: Pencil and paper; the expressway route-planning map and the penalty chart which follow.

NUMBER OF PARTICIPANTS: 4 to 36; preferably at least 12 in order to get 3 groups of 4 each; a group can be made up of 4 or 5 or 6 people.

PROCEDURE:
1. Distribute to each player, called a planner here, an expressway route-planning map and a penalty chart.

2. Explain the map and the penalties. Tell everyone that the symbols on the map represent obstacles that a planner should try to avoid, ideally:

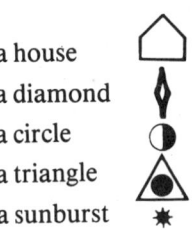

a house   represents a residential area
a diamond   represents a business area
a circle   represents a hill and forest area
a triangle   represents a national historical site
a sunburst   represents an archeological digging site

The planner receives penalty points if his/her expressway route passes through any hexagon showing a symbol—house, diamond, circle, triangle, or sunburst—as determined by the penalty chart (see the penalty chart).

The penalty points for each hexagon depend on (a) the type of symbol, (b) the number of symbols, and (c) the role of the player. That is, if you are a Commuter, then the penalty for passing through one business area is 5 points and twice that if you pass through 2 business areas. However, if you are an Environmentalist, then the penalty for passing through a business area is only 1 point.

Also, there is a 5-point penalty for each hexagon your expressway passes through, whether empty or not. This is in addition to any specific penalty points arising from the symbols in the hexagon. An empty hexagon for a Taxpayer and for everyone else counts 5 points. Thus, for a Taxpayer a hexagon containing 2 houses (3 points each) counts 5 points *plus* 6 points for destroying two houses, for a total of 11 points.

The penalties reflect costs in constructing an expressway. The penalty for passing through a hill and forest area exists because there is added expense in cost when cutting through or leveling a hill. Similarly, the penalty for destroying a residential or business area reflects the expense due to acquiring and razing the structures and relocating the people and organizations. The penalties for 2 hills are more than for one hill because it costs more to cut through the additional hill. The penalty for every hexagon, empty or filled, reflects the fact that the cost of an expressway is also a

Paper, Pencil, Pennies—Like the Real World

function of total mileage. The longer the road the more the cost. It costs more to build a road that wiggles from side to side than one that goes straight.

Penalties are dependent on role in order to reflect special-interest positions. A representative of the Merchants and Manufacturers Association must give particular attention to protect business areas, whereas such a person does not necessarily care to protect archeological digging sites. On the other hand, members of the State Historical Society receive a penalty of 3 points for destroying an archeological digging site because they are expected to protect such areas.

In short, because these are all penalty points, *the lower the score the better.*

3. Assign roles to the players. You may use any combination of the 6 available roles. Determine how many groups of people you wish to have and select the roles you wish to use. It is best to have at least four people in a group. You can have five or six, too. If the number of players is not a multiple of 4, 5, or 6, then pair up some players to play one role. The organizations to be represented are the State Historical Society, the Taxpayers Committee, the Commuters Group, the Merchants and Manufacturers Association, the City Engineer's Office, and the Environmental Club.

4. Ask each player *on his/her own* in light of the assigned role to plot a continuous expressway route from City Hall to any of the 4 empty terminals at the top. The player's goal is to plot a route with a *minimum* of penalty points. Players mark their maps (see page 134) in pencil in order to change routes easily as they go along. On the sides of the map they can calculate their points as they proceed, or they can make tally marks on the penalty chart to keep track of what they have passed through on the map.

5. After all players have individually plotted an expressway route, have the players go to a Negotiation table. At each table there should be one representative of each of the roles used. Thus, with 16 players and 4 in a group there will be 4 Negotiation tables, each with 4 different roles present. Together each group of 4 representatives must plot an expressway route. Obviously, a player will veer away from his/her own route in order to come to a

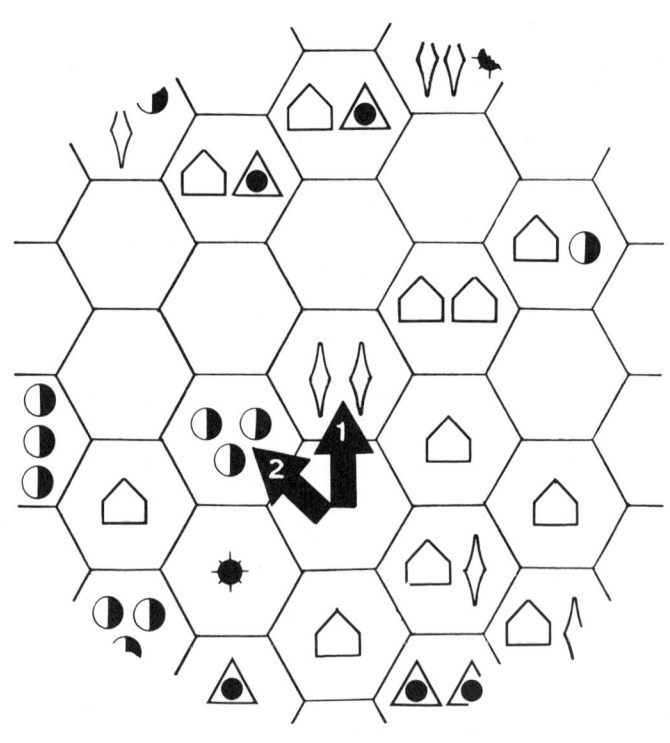

Commuter	City Engineer
1 BAD MOVE	1 GOOD MOVE
2 GOOD MOVE	2 BAD MOVE

compromise route for the table. Yet a player's goal should be to avoid yielding so much that his/her own penalty score increases excessively. Distribute a clean map to each player on which to plot the group's compromise route.

6. After all Negotiation tables have completed their group routes, ask each planner again to calculate his/her score on that route, given his/her role. That is, he/she calculates what the penalty socre is on the group route as a State Historical Society representative, for example. Thus, the same group route will yield different scores for the different roles. Each player will now have 2 scores: one for an individual route and one for a group route according to the assigned role. Ask each Negotiation table to add up the various role scores on the group route in order to arrive at its group score.

7. Regroup the planners for comparison purposes. All players of the same role sit together now. That is, if there are 16 players and 4 roles used, there will be 4 Comparison tables. Players can compare their scores from their individual routes and their group routes.

8. After players have finished their Comparisons, they determine the winners (see the following discussion).

9. Post the results publicly and talk to the planners about what happened. Debriefing is essential. See the Debriefing Hints section.

WINNER: There are several individual winners, one for each role. For example, determine which Commuter representative had the lowest penalty point score in the *group route*. This low score indicates success in negotiations. Do this for all roles. If you wish, you can also have several winners who had the lowest scores on their *individual routes*. Also, determine the winning Negotiation table by determining which table had the lowest sum of all group-route role scores.

Paper, Pencil, Pennies—Like the Real World

Below is chart of a 5-member group that played Expressway. The chart shows the 5 roles with the scores on individually planned routes and the scores for these roles on the group routes. The total group route score of 517, by the way, is not the lowest possible score. One of the other 3 groups that played planned a route that yielded a lower total score of 512. Note the change in scores when the 5 people planned together in order to get agreement on a common route.

	Individual Routes	*Group Route*
State Historical Society	94	101
Taxpayers Commmittee	104	105
Commuters Group	104	107
Merchants and Manufacturers Association	104	105
City Engineer's Office	103	99
Total	509	517

PENALTY CHART FOR EXPRESSWAY ROUTE PLANNING

	RESIDENTIAL AREA ⬠	BUSINESS AREA ◆	HILL & FOREST AREA ◐	NATIONAL HISTORIC SITE ▲	ARCHEOLOGICAL DIGGING SITE ✸
1. STATE HISTORICAL SOCIETY	1	1	1	5	3
2. TAXPAYERS COMMITTEE	3	3	3	1	1
3. COMMUTERS GROUP	3	5	1	1	1
4. MERCHANTS AND MANUFACTURERS ASSOCIATION	1	7	1	1	1
5. CITY ENGINEER'S OFFICE	1	1	7	1	1
6. ENVIRONMENTAL CLUB	1	1	3	3	3

ALSO: 5 PENALTY POINTS FOR EACH HEXAGON PASSED THROUGH (EMPTY OR FILLED), INCLUDING CITY HALL AND TERMINAL HEXAGONS

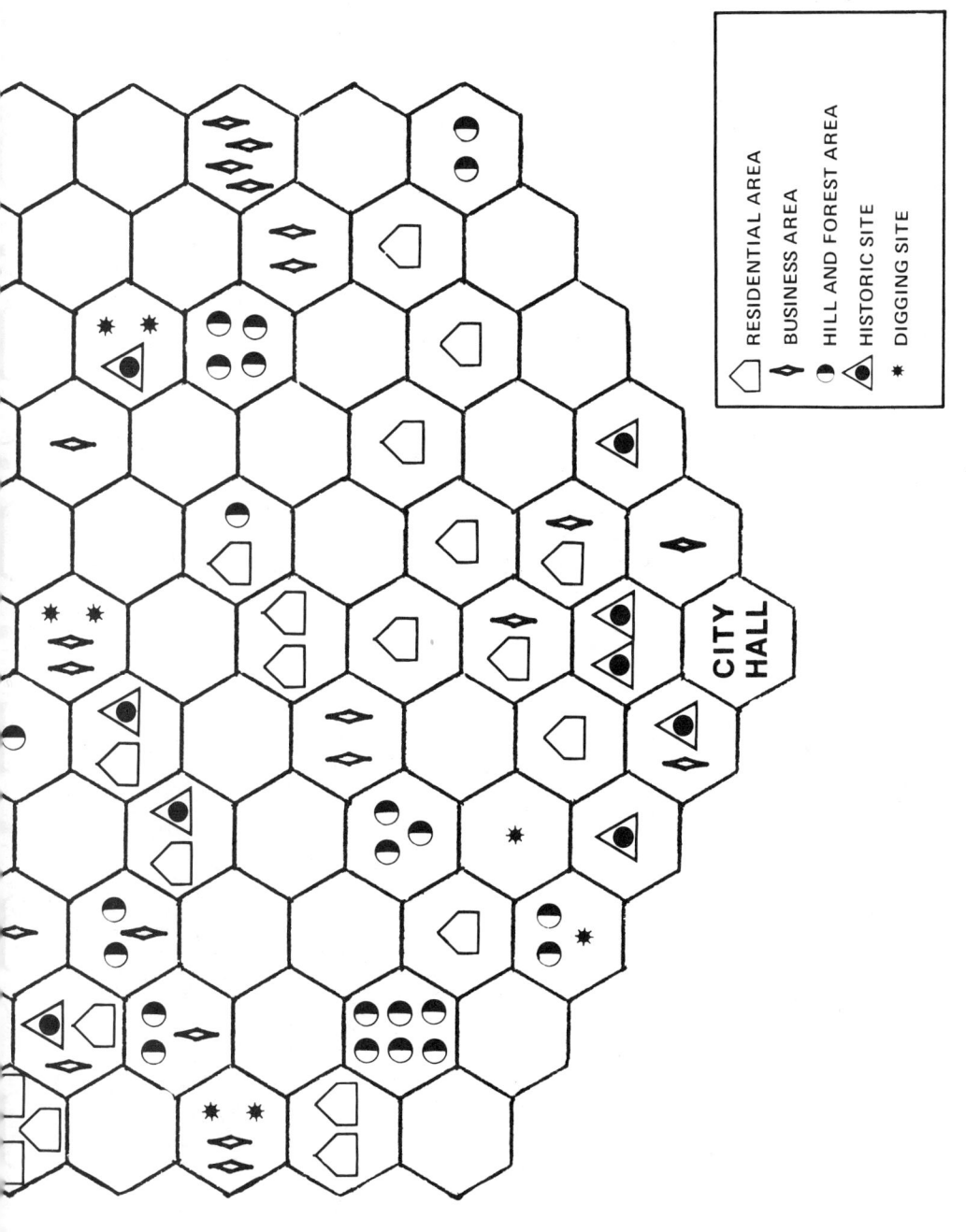

VARIATIONS:
1. Have the players start at the top and end at City Hall.
2. Choose different roles.
3. Make up new roles and penalty points.
4. During Negotiations have players with the same role meet for a short while to discuss their common problems. Then have them return to their respective Negotiation tables to decide on their group routes.
5. Alter the map a bit by adding symbols in selected hexagons.

NOTES/COMMENTS: In the way the Expressway Route-Planning Map is designed, certain roles will naturally have higher penalty scores than others. This is to simulate the fact that often a given special-interest group can find an easy solution to a problem because there are few obstacles it needs to or wishes to consider from its vantage point. The variation in scores, reflecting different expressway routes, is precisely what is needed for a Negotiation table to get the feel of conflicting special interests in community planning activities.

DEBRIEFING HINTS: Talk about the scores achieved by the players of the various roles; who gained and who lost in Negotiations; who had the easiest and who had the toughest task planning an expressway route with the given map; which routes were finally decided on as group routes; what the symbols and hexagons represent in real life; what problems were encountered in Negotiations; how conflicts of interest were resolved; what other community planning tasks are similar to this one of expressway route planning; what guidelines can be offered to negotiators to help them resolve conflicts arising from special interests.

Appendix A
How to Win at NIM

To understand how to play NIM strategically so that you can win, you must understand that in NIM there are "safe" and "unsafe" positions. A safe position means that you form and leave your opponent a position that will guarantee you a win if you continue to play strategically. An unsafe position means that you form and leave your opponent a position from which he/she can guarantee himself/herself a win with strategic play. From a safe position a player can form only an unsafe position. But from an unsafe position a player can form either a safe or an unsafe position. Thus, a player will win if he/she always forms a safe position to leave for the opponent.

Obviously the key lies in knowing whether a position is safe or unsafe. There are two methods to determine a safe position. Both involve math based on 2 and its powers. Both yield the same results.

Method #1 uses binary math and its special notation system. This is a good method to teach if you wish to talk about computers. In binary math, which is computer math, there are only two symbols, 1 and 0. The binary system is but another way of writing numbers with 1 and 0 as the sums of the powers of 2. The binary system uses one column for 2^0, two columns for 2^1, three columns for 2^2, and adds an additional place for each power of 2. The first column on the right stands for 2^0 (which equals 1); the second column from the right stands for 2^1 (which equals 2); the third column stands for 2^2 (which equals 4); the fourth column stands for 2^3 (which equals 8); and so forth. By using the symbols 1 and 0 and adding a column for each power of 2, we can write *every possible number.* For example, here are numbers 1 through 16 as a start in binary math:

DECIMAL	BINARY	MEANING
	168421	
0	0	No 1
1 (-2^0)	1	One 1
2 ($=2^1$)	10	One 2 + No 1
3	11	One 2 + One 1
4 ($=2^2$)	100	One 4 + No 2 + No 1
5	101	One 4 + No 2 + One 1
6	110	One 4 + One 2 + No 1
7	111	One 4 + One 2 + One 1
8 ($=2^3$)	1000	One 8 + No 4 + No 2 + No 1
9	1001	One 8 + No 4 + No 2 + One 1
10	1010	One 8 + No 4 + One 2 + No 1
11	1011	One 8 + No 4 + One 2 + One 1
12	1100	One 8 + One 4 + No 2 + No 1
13	1101	One 8 + One 4 + No 2 + One 1
14	1110	One 8 + One 4 + One 2 + No 1
15	1111	One 8 + One 4 + One 2 + One 1
16 ($=2^4$)	10000	One 16 + No 8 + No 4 + No 2 + No 1

To determine if a position is safe or unsafe in Method #1

a. Convert the number of pennies in each row to a binary number as follows. For example in a game of 3 - 5 - 7, write as follows:

$$3 = 11$$
$$5 = 101$$
$$7 = \underline{111}$$

For 6 - 10 - 13, write as follows:

$$6 = 110$$
$$10 = 1010$$
$$13 = \underline{1101}$$

b. If *each and every* column is "even" (zeroes do not count; only 1's count), then the position is safe. If one or more column is "odd," then the position is unsafe.

c. Therefore, a position of 6 - 10 - 13 is unsafe, as

$$6 = 110$$
$$10 = 1010$$
$$13 = \underline{1101}$$

and the right-hand column is "odd." In a position of 5 - 9 - 12, the position is safe because each and every column is even:

$$5 = 101$$
$$9 = 1001$$
$$12 = \underline{1100}$$

Method #2 is the one I use when I play NIM. Method #1 is an excellent one to use in playing NIM if you have time and the privacy to use pencil and paper for calculating. However, if you wish to calculate *in your head,* then use *Method #2.*

To determine if a position is safe or unsafe in Method #2:

a. Express the number of pennies in each row as the sum of distinct powers of the number 2. The powers of 2 are: 1, 2, 4, 8, 16, 32, 64, and so forth. For example:

$$3 = 2 + 1 \qquad 6 = 4 + 2 \qquad 5 = 4 + 1$$
$$5 = 4 + 1 \qquad 10 = 8 + 2 \qquad 9 = 8 + 1$$
$$7 = 4 + 2 + 1 \qquad 13 = 8 + 4 + 1 \qquad 12 = 8 + 4$$

b. If all the numbers now form pairs, then the position is safe. Thus, 5 - 9 - 12 is safe because there are pairs of 4's, 1's, and 8's and no left-over numbers. But 3 - 5 - 7 and 6 - 10 - 13 are unsafe because not every number is paired off. In each of these two cases there is an extra 1 not part of a pair. One or more extra, unpaired numbers indicates an unsafe position.

Whether you use Method #1 or Method #2 to determine if a position is safe or not, you now proceed in the same way. If the position is unsafe, you remove the correct number of pennies to make it safe. Each column will be "even" if you use Method #1 or every number will be paired off if you use Method #2. Thus in our basic game of 3 - 5 - 7 (an unsafe beginning position) you can form a safe position on your first turn by taking one penny from any row. You can leave 2 - 5 - 7, or 3 - 4 - 7, or 3 - 5 - 6. All these are safe positions as shown by Method #1 and Method #2. From then on, if you continue to play strategically by forming safe positions, you will win.

If the starting position or any subsequent position is safe, you cannot guarantee a win on your move. You should remove only one penny and bide your time until your opponent leaves you an unsafe position accidentally. Then you should form a safe position. Once you form a safe position at any point in a game, you will win if you continue to strategically form and leave safe positions on each turn.

Here is a list of safe positions for our simple, basic game of 3 - 5 - 7. You can verify this list by using either Method #1 or Method #2 or by playing out the game. (Later you can make your own list of safe positions for other starting variations of rows and pennies.)

0-1-1	1-2-3	3-4-7
0-2-2	1-4-5	3-5-6
0-3-3	2-4-6	
0-4-4	2-5-7	
0-5-5		

SAFE POSITIONS IN A NIM GAME OF 3 - 5 - 7

Appendix B

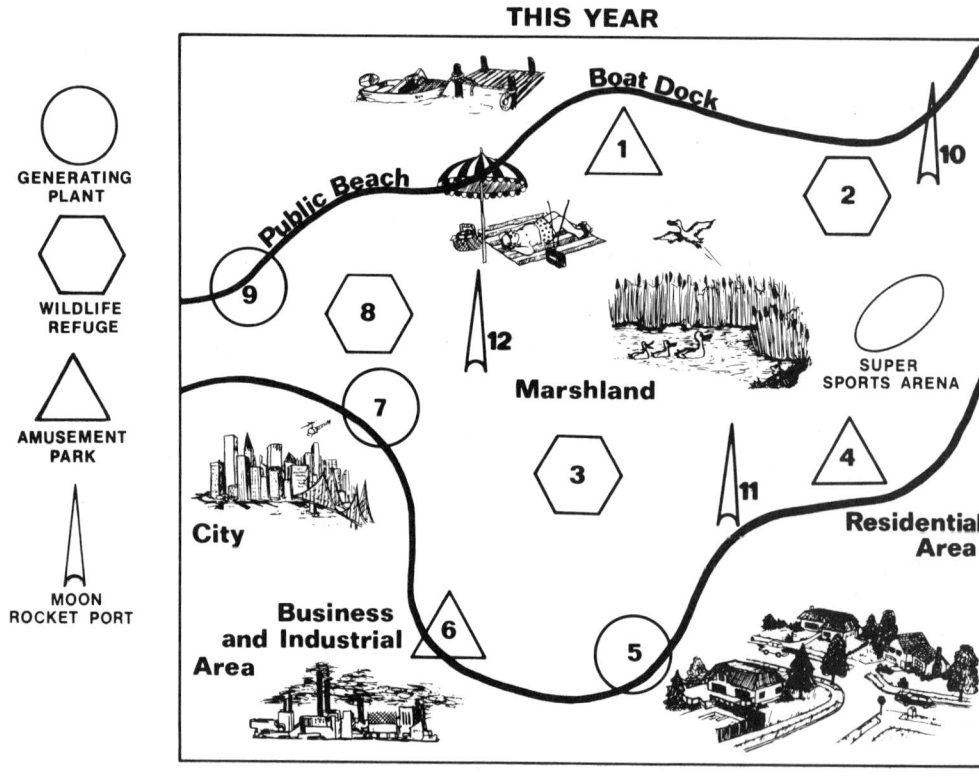

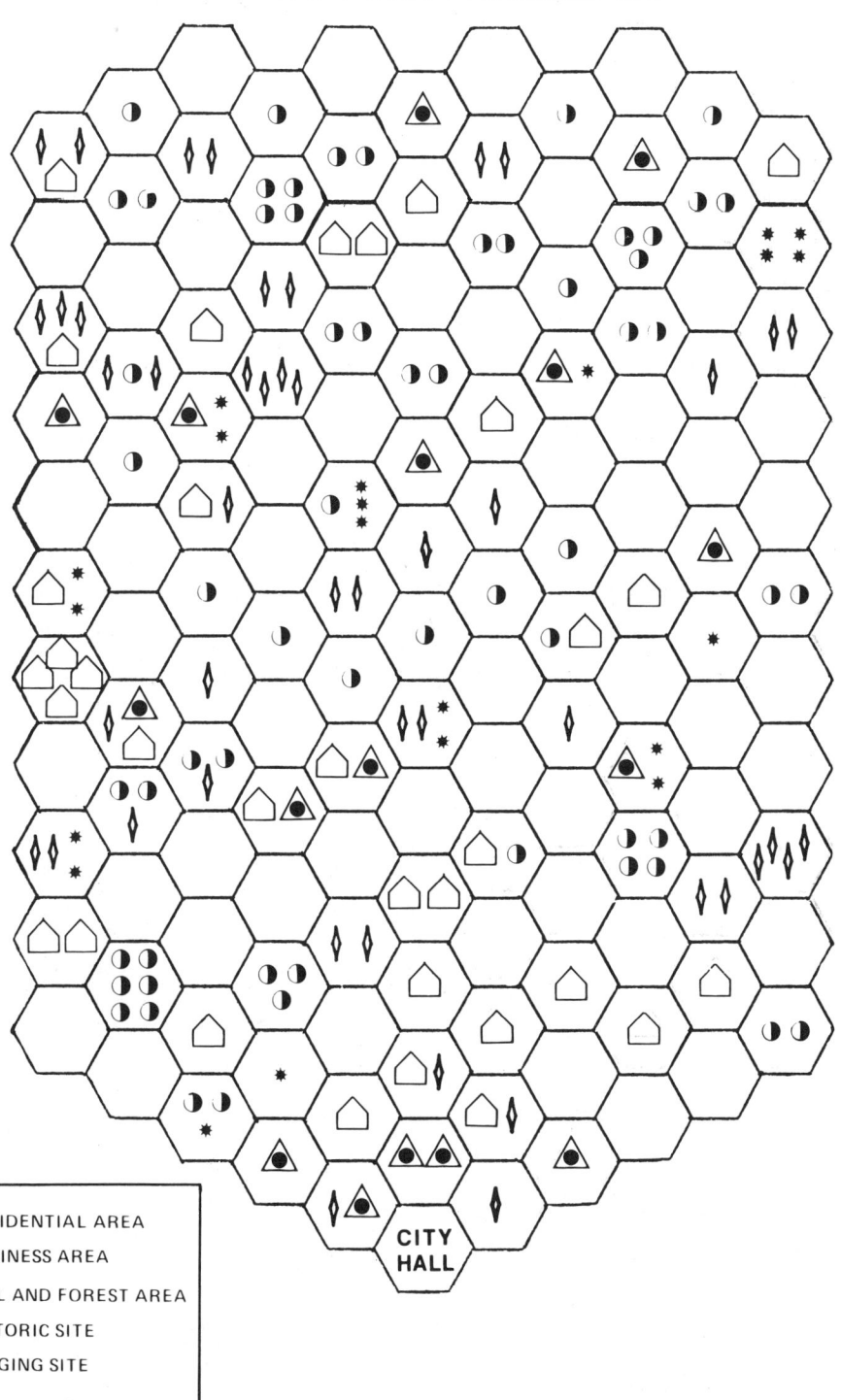